James

AF813475

DAILY SEEDS

James

THE MOVEMENT FROM CASUAL RELIGION TO REAL CHRISTIANITY

J. D. Walt

ZONDERVAN REFLECTIVE

SEEDBED

ZONDERVAN REFLECTIVE

James
Copyright © 2026 by J. D. Walt

Published by Zondervan, 3950 Sparks Drive SE, Suite 101, Grand Rapids, MI 49546, USA. Zondervan is a registered trademark of The Zondervan Corporation, L.L.C., a wholly owned subsidiary of HarperCollins Christian Publishing, Inc.

Requests for information should be addressed to customercare@harpercollins.com.

Zondervan titles may be purchased in bulk for educational, business, fundraising, or sales promotional use. For information, please email SpecialMarkets@Zondervan.com.

ISBN 978-0-310-17174-4 (softcover)
ISBN 978-0-310-17176-8 (audio)
ISBN 978-0-310-17175-1 (ebook)

Unless otherwise noted, Scripture quotations are taken from The Holy Bible, New International Version®, NIV®. Copyright © 1973, 1978, 1984, 2011 by Biblica, Inc. Used by permission of Zondervan. All rights reserved worldwide. www.Zondervan.com.

Scripture quotations marked ESV are from the ESV® Bible (The Holy Bible, English Standard Version®), © 2001 by Crossway, a publishing ministry of Good News Publishers. ESV Text Edition: 2025. The ESV text may not be quoted in any publication made available to the public by a Creative Commons license. The ESV may not be translated in whole or in part into any other language. Used by permission. All rights reserved.

Scripture quotations marked MSG are taken from The Message. Copyright © 1993, 2002, 2018 by Eugene H. Peterson. Used by permission of NavPress. All rights reserved. Represented by Tyndale House Publishers.

Any internet addresses (websites, blogs, etc.) and telephone numbers in this book are offered as a resource. They are not intended in any way to be or imply an endorsement by Zondervan, nor does Zondervan vouch for the content of these sites and numbers for the life of this book.

All rights reserved. No part of this publication may be reproduced, stored in a retrieval system, or transmitted in any form or by any means—electronic, mechanical, photocopy, recording, or any other—except for brief quotations in printed reviews, without the prior permission of the publisher.

Without limiting the exclusive rights of any author, contributor or the publisher of this publication, any unauthorized use of this publication to train generative artificial intelligence (AI) technologies is expressly prohibited. HarperCollins also exercise their rights under Article 4(3) of the Digital Single Market Directive 2019/790 and expressly reserve this publication from the text and data mining exception.

HarperCollins Publishers, Macken House, 39/40 Mayor Street Upper, Dublin 1, D01 C9W8, Ireland (https://www.harpercollins.com)

Cover design and illustration: Derek Thornton / Notch Design
Series design: Derek Thornton / Notch Design
Interior design: Denise Froehlich

Printed in the United States of America

26 27 28 29 30 LBC 5 4 3 2 1

To the late Mrs. Betty Jane Oldner,
my first real Christian,
who taught me how to stand on the Word of God.
May your tribe increase—
on earth as it is in heaven!

Contents

Week 4: James 3:9–4:12

Week 5: James 4:13–5:20

Preface

What are the two most important words of the day? I'm glad you asked. My take: the first word and the last word. Who gets the first word in your day? Who gets the last word? I have a confession: I have realized my slow drift into giving Instagram the first word of my day. It was simple and benign—just a quick scroll through the photos my friends posted over the last half day or so. Then this realization: Netflix was getting the last word of my day. Before drifting off to sleep, I would watch the next episode of some show that had caught my attention along the way. First word: *Instagram*. Last word: *Netflix*.

Days become weeks. Weeks become months. Months become years. And days, weeks, months, and years become us. Our lives consist not in the big decisions and banner events dotting our calendars, but in the little things we consistently do day after day after day. We are what we do . . . every single day.

Each one of us has within our stewardship the ability to decide who will get the first and last words in our life. You know where this is headed. But first let me tell you what happened with my Instagram -Netflix ways. The problem is that I want to make Instagram and Netflix the problem when they aren't the problem. The problem is with me and the misspent priority of my own heart. So I didn't decide to delete Instagram and swear off Netflix. Instead, I decided I would shift the priority of my heart. I determined to give the Word of God the first word and the last word of my days.

Though my day may be filled with a thousand distractions and a hundred course corrections, it is now determined—my day will be framed by, surrounded with, enclosed in the Word of God. First Word. Last Word. God's Word.

> The grass withers and the flowers fall,
> but the word of our God endures forever. (Isaiah 40:8)

Consider the stark simplicity and brazen boldness of this word from the prophet Isaiah. Everything is ephemeral. Only one thing is eternal—the Word of God.

Next to the front door of our home, the one we enter and exit through almost every time, is a chalkboard. And on the chalkboard are written those words. I read that verse at least once every single day. I say it aloud so my ears can hear it. Can I possibly be reminded enough that everything around me is passing away save one thing—the Word of God? Can I possibly be encouraged enough to come to Jesus and have him build my life on the singular enduring reality of the Word of God? First Word. Last Word. God's Word.

I offer you an invitation through this book to journey with me and others to shift the priority of your heart and mind. Each day we will gather around a biblical text. We will invite the text of Scripture to speak both the first and the last word of our day. Write some of the text for the day in a journal or on a note card, a whiteboard, or a chalkboard, and make it a simple act of worship to read it aloud each morning as the first word of the day and also at the close as the last word of the day.

Along the way we will reflect together on how to increase the priority, prominence, and integration of the Word of God in our everyday lives. If we will give ourselves to the gentle work of this way of walking together, I suspect we will find pathways of delight and devotion winding through the wilderness of this world and the sanctuaries of our own souls that we never imagined existed. And something tells me these First-Word-Last-Word-God's-Word paths will find their way into tomorrow and next week and next month and onward, until they have become our lives.

Now I'm going to say, "The grass withers and the flowers fall," and you are going to say, "but the word of our God endures forever."

J. D. Walt

How This Works

This is a different kind of Bible study. The Bible is both the source and the subject. And you will learn information about the Bible along the way, such as its history, context, original languages, and authors. The goal is not educational in nature, but transformational. We will focus more on knowing Jesus than on knowing *about* Jesus.

To that end, each reading begins with the definitive inspiration of the Holy Spirit, the ongoing, unfolding text of Scripture. Following that is a short and hopefully substantive insight into the text and some aspect of its meaning. For insight to lead to deeper influence, we turn the text into prayer. Finally, influence must run its course toward impact. This is why you will find questions at the end of each chapter. These questions are designed not to elicit information but to crystallize intention.

Discipleship always leads from inspiration to attention, from attention to intention, and from intention to action.

Committing to Everyday Reading and Prayer

While Scripture always addresses us personally, it is not written to us individually. The content of Scripture cries out for a community of listeners and readers. This resource is designed for discipleship in community. You could read this like a traditional book—a few pages or chapters at a time. You could cram the readings the night before a group meeting. Those ways of reading are not the intention of this book. Keep in mind, Daily Seeds is not called *Daily* Seeds for kicks. We believe Scripture is worthy of our most focused and consistent attention. Every day. We all have misses, but let's make daily reading and prayer more than a noble aspiration; let's make it our covenant with one another.

This discipleship tool will create spiritual habits of individual reading and of praying the biblical text—six days on your own and one day with others.

How to Use with Small Groups

Daily Seeds is a proven discipleship resource that works in a variety of contexts—from churches studying a book of the Bible together to small groups to Sunday school classes to virtual meetings. Assuming your group meets weekly, group and class members should read one chapter every day. You will notice there is not an assigned reading for the seventh day. On the seventh day, meet with your group to share, pray, and encourage one another with insights or struggles that the text brought up in you during the previous six days. Use the following guidelines to help structure your group meetings as you allow Scripture to transform you in community.

The guidelines for using Daily Seeds in small groups or class settings are meant to be simple. Perhaps share the responsibility of leading group meetings. Remember that the goal is transformation.

1. Hearing the Text

Invite the group to settle into silence for a period of no less than one and no more than five minutes. Ask an appointed person to keep time and to read the biblical text covering the period of days since the last group meeting. Allow at least one minute of silence following the reading of the text.

2. Responding to the Text

Invite anyone from the group to respond to the reading by answering these prompts: What did you hear? What did you see? What did you otherwise sense from the Lord?

3. Sharing Insights and Implications for Discipleship

Moving in an orderly rotation (or free-for-all), invite people to share insights and implications from the week's readings. What did you find challenging, encouraging, provocative, comforting, invasive, inspiring, corrective, affirming, guiding, or warning? Allow group conversation to proceed at will. Limit to one sharing item per turn, with multiple rounds of discussion.

4. Shaping Intentions for Prayer

Invite each person in the group to share a single discipleship intention for the week ahead. It is helpful if this goal for growing in discipleship can also be framed as a question the group can use to check in from the prior week. At each person's turn, they are invited to share how their intention went during the previous week. The class or group can open and close the meeting according to its established patterns.

Introduction

I sometimes buy books for the title. You too? The other day I came across one too good to pass up. Be warned; it's long—not the book, but the title: *A Practical View of the Prevailing Religious System of Professed Christians, in the Higher and Middle Classes in This Country, Contrasted with Real Christianity.* Wow! Just wow! The real kicker comes in when you see who wrote it. Does the name William Wilberforce ring a bell? Yes, this is the same William Wilberforce who famously said, "You may choose to look the other way, but you can never say again you did not know."[1]

He took on the slave trade of the eighteenth century, mobilizing an abolitionist movement we marvel at to the present day. He once remarked, "To live our lives and miss that great purpose we were designed to accomplish is truly a sin. It is inconceivable that we could be bored in a world with so much wrong to tackle, so much ignorance to teach and so much misery we could alleviate."[2]

Reflecting on his own life and abolitionist passion during a speech in the House of Commons on May 12, 1789, he commented, "So enormous, so dreadful, so irremediable did the [slave] trade's wickedness appear that my own mind was completely made up for abolition. Let the consequences be what they would; I from this time determined that I would never rest until I had effected its abolition."[3]

---

1. Quoted in Loren Skinker, "Slavery and the Gospel: William Wilberforce 261 Years Later," ABWE, accessed October 20, 2025, https://abwe.org/blog/slavery-and-gospel-william-wilberforce-261-years-later/.
2. William Wilberforce, *Real Christianity: A Paraphrase in Modern English of* A Practical View of the Prevailing Religious System of Professed Christians, in the Higher and Middle Classes in This Country, Contrasted with Real Christianity, rev. Bob Beltz (Regal, 2006), 71. A classic originally published in 1797.
3. Schomburg Center for Research in Black Culture, Manuscripts, Archives and Rare Books Division, New York Public Library, "Speeches in Parliament, Respecting the Abolition of the African Slave Trade," *New York Public Library Digital Collections*, accessed

In an age of profound blight and a church of passive slumber, Wilberforce rose up as a real Christian. When it came to taking on slavery, he was willing to go first.

This is how I think of James, the brother of Jesus, too. He stepped forward, put his money where his mouth was, and called the followers of Jesus to stop phoning it in. James is an agent of awakening. His life and words operate like a reverse snooze bar. As we start to drift into sleep, he is a wake-up call.

After scarcely saying hello, he offers, "Consider it pure joy, my brothers and sisters, whenever you face trials of many kinds" (1:2).

How about this one? "Do not merely listen to the word, and so deceive yourselves. Do what it says" (1:22). He caps off the first chapter with this: "Religion that God our Father accepts as pure and faultless is this: to look after orphans and widows in their distress and to keep oneself from being polluted by the world" (v. 27).

James and Will would have been good friends. In chapter 2, James cuts to the core, letting us know in no uncertain terms that "faith without deeds is dead" (v. 26). He settled for nothing less than the genuine article. I think of him as the first real Christian.

To be clear, the opposite of a real Christian is not a non-Christian, but rather a nominal Christian. Nominal Christians present big problems for the church—people who claim the name but can't play the game. To be first doesn't necessarily mean the first in sequence, but rather first in kind. We all know people who qualify as first real Christians. Think about it. Who was the first real Christian in your life?

I remember her. Mrs. Betty Jane was old the first time I met her, yet in all the years I knew her, she never got older. She ran a furniture store down on Main Street in my hometown of Dumas, Arkansas. As a young person, I stopped in often to say hello. She would always greet me with the same question: "John David, what Scripture are you standing on today?" She always knew hers. She read the whole Bible through every year from cover to cover and wrote at least as much in the margins as was already on the pages. And she probably loaned more money to poor

---

September 24, 2025, https://digitalcollections.nypl.org/items/e4c179a0-2865-0133-fdf1-60f81dd2b63c.

people without expectation of repayment than her store brought in from sales. She would often remind me, "John David, you can't know the will of God if you don't know the Word of God." Mrs. Betty Jane and James would have been friends.

I remember another first from my early days as a youth pastor trying to herd a throng of loving reprobates well before I knew myself as one of them. Lydia was the first real Christian I came across in those early days of ministry. More than Sunday school answers, she knew Jesus. The great thing about first real Christians is they have a way of almost effortlessly reproducing themselves. Not seconds and thirds, but more firsts.

I remember Lissa, Gretchen, Blair, Christy, Blue, and John Mark, and on I could go. I will never forget Dan, the first real Christian young man who came into the picture. Unlike anything I had ever witnessed at the time, his exuberant faith proved to be a force multiplier. Dan's love of Jesus was personal, powerful, and public. We've all seen people who wear their faith like clothes that don't fit. Dan donned faith, hope, and love like a perfectly tailored three-piece suit, though he wouldn't have been caught dead in a suit. One day, he made a comment in passing that he likely does not remember, but I will never forget. It has come to capture some of the essence for me of what growing up in faith means. He said, "J. D., it's like every time the Lord does something new in my life, I look back and wonder if I was even a Christian before." Here is another first real Christian that James would have loved. My job quickly became holding the door for the likes of these kids and their friends as the Holy Spirit swept through their schools and awakened our whole church.

These first real Christians are not common, but they are everywhere. Anybody who is willing to step up to the plate can be one. Only one person can be first in the world. In the kingdom of God, anyone can be first who is willing to be last. From Francis of Assisi and Francis Asbury to Rosa Parks and Martin Luther King Jr., to be a real Christian means you have to be first—and to be first means to be last. A real Christian doesn't just believe the Word of God; he or she develops a track record for doing it over and over and over again. It's not complicated, yet it's not easy either. James will train us in the ways of real Christians—what it means to be faithful, available, and obedient.

As we journey through the book of James together, he will implore us day after day to become real Christians. We have people (and situations) in our lives who are waiting on the first real Christian to arrive. There are many people all around us who have been hurt by hypocrisy and who will only be healed by seeing the genuine article. They are looking for the first real Christian. Widows, orphans, and so many caught in the cruelty of inescapable poverty wake up every day with hopes of meeting their first real Christian. Jesus has all their numbers, and James has ours. He's looking for more friends like us. Let's join him and add to his tribe of the first real Christians.

1

WEEK

James 1:1–12

1 James 1:1

James, Just James

James

Consider This

James—that's our text today.

James, just James—his name is an inspired word from God to us.

So who was James?

James is one of the most important leaders in the early church. It sounds odd to say such a thing, as most of us (present company included) have given James, the man, so little thought. We've read his book, likely been challenged by the gut punches of his exhortations, and moved on to the more pastoral pastures of greener grass and stiller waters in other parts of the Bible.

After all, the rock stars of the New Testament are clearly Matthew, Mark, Luke, John, Peter, Paul, and Mary. James hardly merits honorable mention among such characters, so our thinking goes. Why? James carries with him some inconvenient truths for the church. For starters, he is the (half) brother of Jesus, a small fact that large parts of the church would rather sweep under the rug, as it glaringly contradicts certain other doctrines about the mother of Jesus.

Then there's the celebrated saint of the Reformation, Martin Luther, who rediscovered the great doctrine of salvation by grace through faith and not by works. While James's signature teaching that "faith without deeds is dead" in no way contradicts the biblical doctrine of justification (i.e., salvation by grace through faith), Luther considered it an affront to the gospel and famously regarded James's work to be an "epistle of straw,"[1] arguing at one point that it had no place in the Bible.

So how can I refer to James as perhaps the most important leader in the early church? James was the earliest leader of the most significant

1. Martin Luther, *Word and Sacrament*, in *Luther's Works* 35 (Muhlenberg, 1960), 362.

church—the church in Jerusalem. The universal church was birthed in Jerusalem. From Jerusalem, the word of God proceeded to the nations. When the debate came over whether and how Gentiles (i.e., most of us) could become part of the church, they called the first council of the church to convene in Jerusalem (see Acts 15). And yes, it was James who voiced the gracious motion to allow the Gentiles' entry into the church without the deal-breaking requirement of circumcision, and with only minimal observances of the Mosaic law (i.e., no sexual immorality, no eating food polluted by idols, no eating blood, etc.). Without the Spirit -anointed leadership of James, the Jewish brother of the Jewish Jesus, the church at Rome might never have gotten off the ground. I'm not knocking Peter, but I do wonder what the church might look like today if we had considered James as our first pope.

While it's a bit more speculative to ponder, James is one of the few people in the history of the world who could shed light on the mysteriously hidden growing-up years of his brother Jesus—what it actually looked like for the Son of God to grow "in wisdom and stature, and in favor with God and man" (Luke 2:52). While James's lips are sealed on the subject, we can be assured he disciples us with this most rarified unwritten commentary running in the background of his imagination.

While much of the New Testament concerns itself with the general spread of the gospel, James offers us something of an advanced course in discipleship—the real Christianity, where the proverbial rubber meets the road of faith. He will not pander to the easy believism of our time. Rather than coddle us in our catastrophes, James will challenge our loyalty to Jesus to the very core of our being as we find ourselves right in the middle of them. I picture James as more Nick Saban and less Mr. Rogers, and more Dr. Laura, less Oprah.

And maybe that's more what we need in these times in which we live. Have we assumed wrongly that seekers seek to be spoon-fed the faith? What if they are looking for the bare, naked truth? What if it's more clear-cut discipleship they seek rather than more new-member classes? (And speaking of testing our assumptions, we will get to more of those soon.)

Maybe the skyrocketing of the "nones" says more about us than them—that "none" doesn't mean somehow bereft of faith, but rather more akin to "we will have *none* of what you are trying to pass off as the church." As American culture grows more hostile to the Christian faith and less hospitable to the church, we will undoubtedly begin to witness something of a threshing floor arise in our midst—a place where the proverbial wheat gets separated from the chaff.

James is not writing to some advanced class of Christians. He's giving us real Christianity, not as a doctrinal treatise, but as basic discipleship. James offers us faith with deeds, mercy with justice, grace with truth, and love with conviction. These are not dichotomies we hold in tension; they are realities we hold in union.

Okay, I'm getting carried away, so I'll leave you with the potent words of the late G. K. Chesterton, who famously wrote, "The Christian ideal has not been tried and found wanting. It has been found difficult; and left untried."[2]

James, just James—his name is an inspired word from God to us.

Somewhere in the future this is all that will remain of us: our name—the story it signifies, the truth it tells, and the legacy it leaves, or not. No matter where we find ourselves in life's ever-changing trials and triumphs, we must be ever turning our ways into the way of Jesus. Though Jesus is the same yesterday and today and forever, he is ever on the move. Far from a static decision, following Jesus is a constant movement. No matter how little or how long, how well or wrongly, we have followed him, may this year be known to the history of our name as the "year of the great turning" to the God and Father of our Lord Jesus Christ.

The Prayer

God our Father, we thank you for James—for his guts, his grit, and his gall to say things to us no one else will. Thank you that he leads us to the real Jesus, whom we must have if we are to ever be like him. We pray in Jesus' name. Amen.

2. G. K. Chesterton, *What's Wrong with the World* (Dodd, Mead, 1910), 61.

The Questions

What if we ceased thinking of going deeper in our discipleship as though it were some kind of option? What if there were only growing and not growing, following Jesus and not following Jesus? What would the implications be for you?

Do you have a James kind of person in your life or in your past? What do you remember about him or her? What was his or her influence on you?

Are you ready to say, "Be it therefore resolved, I will turn to Jesus no matter what"? What action will most seal and communicate that conviction to you?

2

James 1:1

The Problem with My Social Media Bio

James, a servant of God and of the Lord Jesus Christ

Consider This

If you looked at the brief bio I put at the bottom of my social media accounts a few years ago, you would have seen the following: "J. D. Walt. Farmer. Poet. Jurist. Theologian. Publisher."

I'm not sure what I was trying to do with the bio other than to make people think I must be amazing. And here's my big point: It never occurred to me that I might describe myself with the words "a servant of God and of the Lord Jesus Christ."

At the same time, I can't imagine James saying something like "James. Professional fisherman. Movement leader. Brother of Jesus, but Joseph is my real father."

For James, it came down to one thing:

servant of God and of the Lord Jesus Christ

Years ago, my friend Dr. David Hill gave me one of the last business cards of his father, the late Sam Hill, who was a minister in the Church of Christ. Underneath his name were the words "bondslave of Jesus Christ." It struck me so deeply that not only have I never forgotten it, but I have treasured the card in my keepsakes.

Paul instructs us to "have the same mindset as Christ Jesus: Who, being in very nature God, . . . [took on] the very nature of a servant" (see Philippians 2:5–11).

He and other apostles followed suit:

> Paul, a servant of Christ Jesus, called to be an apostle and set apart for the gospel of God. (Romans 1:1)

> Jude, a servant of Jesus Christ and a brother of James. (Jude 1)

> Simon Peter, a servant and apostle of Jesus Christ. (2 Peter 1:1)

> The revelation from Jesus Christ, which God gave him to show his servants what must soon take place. He made it known by sending his angel to his servant John. (Revelation 1:1)

The New Testament teaches us we have two choices when it comes to our bio: We can be a slave of sin or a slave of God. Hear Paul on this: "But now that you have been set free from sin and have become slaves of God, the benefit you reap leads to holiness, and the result is eternal life" (Romans 6:22).

To fail to choose means we will be slaves of sin. In short, slavery to sin simply means to be the servant of oneself. We've surely all discovered by now the deception of thinking we are somehow serving others, when in actuality it's more about how it benefits us. In other words, most of us aren't averse to some form of helping other people. The problem is our servanthood rarely gets beyond some form of our own self-interest—that's the test of true servanthood. How am I benefiting? When Jesus invites us to deny ourselves and take up our cross

(Mark 8:34), he doesn't mean to grit our teeth and bear it; he's talking about the arduous journey toward the joyful abandonment of our self -interestedness. This is precisely what God, in Jesus Christ, has done for us. We express our gratitude to him as we embrace his willingness to work transformation in us for the sake of others. This is what it means to be a "servant of the Lord Jesus Christ."

As much as we may not want to believe it, as human beings, we have a master. Our master will be sin or it will be Jesus Christ. The amazing grace of the gospel is this: In becoming slaves of God, we set our feet on the only road to freedom.

The bigger truth? Freedom is the rediscovery and reclamation of our deepest identity as the beloved, blood-purchased sons and daughters of God. The pathway of discipleship leads us out of our inbred slavery to sin and into claiming our birthright as sons and daughters, into the pure, liberated reality of our life's work—to be the glorious servants of God and the Lord Jesus Christ.

The Prayer

God our Father, I am so self-interested. I see myself primarily through the lens of my shame and my success. Lead me to see myself as your son or daughter so that I might become the kind of person who can truly serve others for their sake and not my own. In Jesus' name. Amen.

The Questions

Try this: I, (insert your name) ________________, am a slave of ________________. (The choices are slave of sin or slave of Jesus Christ.)

Perhaps you feel the deep discontentment of being caught somewhere between these choices. Are you ready to do something about this? It begins with the declaration of who you will become. Are you ready to declare, in the name of Jesus and in the power of the Holy Spirit, "I am a slave of Jesus Christ"? If not, why not?

Speak this aloud: "I am a slave of Jesus Christ." If you are not prepared to do so, try saying aloud, "I am a slave of sin." What effect did this have on you?

3

James 1:1

Why There's No Such Thing as a Christian Nation

James, a servant of God and the Lord Jesus Christ, to the twelve tribes scattered among the nations.

Consider This

Is there such a thing as a Christian nation? Well, yes and no. Let's begin with no.

No, there is no such thing as a Christian nation. Before you denounce me and stop reading, ask yourself, *What would a Christian nation be?* A particular parcel of land? Could Tennessee be a Christian state? Is it the constitution or the governing structures that make a state or nation Christian? Is it the oaths a leader swears (a practice that the Bible seems to forbid) in the name of God that makes a nation Christian? Would it be that a majority of the people in a nation subscribe in some capacity to some form of the Christian religion that makes a nation Christian? We read regularly of territories, regions, or nations declaring themselves to be an Islamic state. And they don't seem to need a majority. Would a Christian state just be a different form of what they are talking about?

So maybe if all the laws and ordinances in a given nation were taken exactly and explicitly from the Bible, and its leaders were ordained by God to carry out the governance of such a place, we might be getting closer to some concept of a Christian nation; however, is this not getting close to the idea of the church? Was this country not founded, at least in part, on the wishes of its people to escape from a state run by the church, which almost invariably becomes a church run by the state? When people speak of America being founded as a Christian nation, they mean that many of its founders and early leaders were real Christians, and they acted accordingly, as only a real Christian can do.

No, I don't think a nation can be properly considered a Christian nation. So why did I answer the question as both yes and no? I believe that the only entity that actually can be Christian is a human being, and that a nation can only be Christian to the extent that its people are, in fact, real Christians.

What do I mean by "real Christians"? Thanks for asking. That's exactly where James comes in, and what James is all about. As I mentioned in the introduction, I recently picked up a book I had never heard of, written by William Wilberforce. The title says it all: *A Practical View of the Prevailing Religious System of Professed Christians, in the Middle and Higher Classes in this Country, Contrasted with Real Christianity.* Don't you wish we had book titles like this one today?

Now back to James. He identifies his audience as follows:

> to the twelve tribes scattered among the nations.

James is not writing to a Christian nation; he is writing to Jewish Christians scattered among the nations. Rather than writing to America as a Christian nation, I think he might write to the church of Jesus Christ scattered among the nation of the United States of America. I don't see James exhorting the scattered tribes to take back the nations for Christ. He's not urging anyone to smite the infidels. He is pleading with so-called Christians to become *real Christians*. James is looking for true religion.

The problem we have in the United States (and in almost every other nation on earth) is that we don't have enough real Christians. It is because of the failure of so-called Christians to be real Christians that we now have a disastrous welfare state trying to take care of the widows, orphans, poor, and aging. The failure of America (or any other nation) will not be laid at the feet of the nonbelievers. The success of America (or any other nation) will not come as a result of Christians somehow taking back the nation, as though the nonbelievers were our enemies. The future of the nations will depend entirely on the spreading of the gospel of Jesus Christ and the advancement of the kingdom of God. This will happen only to the extent that our churches cease trading our birthright for a pot of middle- and upper-class suburban stew.

There are no Christian nations—only one Christian nation that constitutes the people of God. Peter said it best: "You are a chosen people, a royal priesthood, a holy nation, God's special possession, that you may declare the praises of him who called you out of darkness into his wonderful light" (1 Peter 2:9).

When James talks to the twelve tribes scattered among the nations, that's what he means. Let's determine to take this very personally.

The Prayer

God our Father, forgive us for delegating the responsibility of being Christian to some nation, group, or organization when only we can be Christians. I want to be a real Christian. Come, Holy Spirit, and lead me in this way. In Jesus' name. Amen.

The Questions

What do you think about this idea of no such thing as a Christian nation?

Are you ready to begin (or deepen) your praying for a great awakening in our land, so that Christ followers turn away from so-called Christianity to real Christianity?

Where do you find yourself these days? Are you a comfortable Christian content with middle- to upper-class prosperity, or are you dissatisfied with the prevailing status quo of how the Christian faith has come to be practiced?

4

James 1:2–4

The Difference Between Your Perseverance and the Holy Spirit's Perseverance

Consider it pure joy, my brothers and sisters, whenever you face trials of many kinds, because you know that the testing of your faith produces perseverance. Let perseverance finish its work so that you may be mature and complete, not lacking anything.

Consider This

Is James serious? View our worst problems as a gift?

This advice actually sounds really good until you have a test or challenge in front of you. Think about the text this way: "Consider it a sheer gift, friends, when you get diagnosed with cancer, when you have to declare bankruptcy, when you just lost your job, or when you just got served divorce papers."

Really? A sheer gift? A gift is supposed to be something good —something you want for Christmas or your birthday. A gift is supposed to be something the Holy Spirit graces you with for blessing other people. How can dark days, hard times, and deep distress be a gift?

James is training us to perceive the world like Christ. He's not saying these tests and challenges are great things that we want more of in our lives. He's saying it's just going to happen. We can count on tests and challenges coming our way, especially if we are trying to follow Jesus. Didn't Jesus say as much? "In this world you will have trouble. But take heart! I have overcome the world" (John 16:33).

Jesus and James teach us we must change our mind as it relates to tests, challenges, and overall hard times. To "consider" something, as the text instructs, means to change the way you approach it. It's like counting one's weakness as strength or counting a loss as a gain.

Do you remember these words from Philippians 2:5–7: "Have the same mindset as Christ Jesus: Who, being in very nature God, did not consider equality with God something to be used to his own advantage; rather, he made himself nothing"? That's what James is getting at.

Do you remember where Paul put it like this in Philippians 2:3: "Do nothing from selfish ambition or conceit, but in humility count others more significant than yourselves" (ESV)? That's what James means.

In Philippians 3:8, Paul put it this way: "What is more, I consider everything a loss because of the surpassing worth of knowing Christ Jesus my Lord, for whose sake I have lost all things. I consider them garbage, that I may gain Christ." James is not asking us to call what is true "false" or what is false "true." No, he's inviting us into the deeper wisdom of the mind of Christ. More on that in the next chapter.

Wisdom defies conventional thinking. Wisdom often leads us to a completely counterintuitive way of approaching life—you know, like when Jesus said the least among us is the greatest, and the last will be considered the first (Luke 9:48; Matthew 20:16). James is schooled in the mind of Jesus, and he's inviting us inside.

The way we consider tests and challenges will determine the outcome they produce in our lives. Tests and challenges can either ruin people or renovate them. It cannot be overstressed how much the Christian faith depends on a changed or renewed mind. Faith is not about our ever-changing feelings. Our feelings can be a great gift or a total distraction. Faith is about the mind, and when I say *mind*, I don't mean *brain*. When Scripture speaks of the mind, it speaks of the central core of one's personhood—the place where heart, strength, spirit, body, intellect, soul, and will converge. It's why Scripture instructs us to "have the same mindset as Christ Jesus" (Philippians 2:5) or to "not conform to the pattern of this world, but be transformed by the renewing of your mind" (Romans 12:2).

Why must we change our mind with respect to how we consider tests and trials in our life?

> . . . because you know that the testing of your faith produces perseverance. Let perseverance finish its work so that you may be mature and complete, not lacking anything.

It's important to note that Christian discipleship is not training in how to be a stoic. It's not about how one reacts to trials, but rather about how one is willing to be broken by God in the midst of them. Again, note the distinction—not broken by the trials, but broken by God in the midst of trials. To be broken by God means to be healed of our broken and willful ways of dealing with life. To be broken by God means to finally come to the place where we can admit that we do not have what it takes—that we have exhausted our resources, are at the end of our rope, and are poor in spirit. It means to finally be brought to the place where we are ready for an entirely new way of living life—God's way.

Perseverance does not mean grinding away or gutting it out in our own strength. Perseverance, in the mindset of Christ, means laying down our strength so that the strength of the Holy Spirit can rise up within us—not in spite of our weakness, but because of it. Perseverance is not something we do, but rather it's something the Holy Spirit does in us. His work of creating endurance in us is excruciatingly hard but inestimably good, which is why we are able to count our trials as "pure joy." I mean, who does not want this outcome: "so that you may be mature and complete, not lacking anything." That is God's agenda in our trials and tests. We can trust him.

The difference between your perseverance and the Holy Spirit's perseverance within you is all the difference in the world.

The Prayer

God our Father, help me to be thankful for my trials, not because of them, but because of you. This is where you meet me best, where I need you most. I feel so far away from this kind of faith. Come, Holy Spirit, and cause me to move from my feelings to the facts of faith, where I can consider it pure joy to face hard times, for then I will more truly face you. In Jesus' name. Amen.

The Questions

James was writing within the context of serious economic challenges for the people he addressed. What context is he writing about within your life? In other words, what are your tests and trials at the moment?

Are there tests and trials in your past you can now look back on and see how God used them to create maturity in your life and faith?

What difference do you see in grinding it out through your trials and allowing yourself to be broken by God in the midst of them? Can you see the difference between a stoic determination and a surrendered disposition?

Can you distinguish between your own strength of spirit to persevere and the Holy Spirit's perseverance within you?

5

James 1:5–8

Why Faith Is Not the Opposite of Doubt—and What Actually Is

> *If any of you lacks wisdom, you should ask God, who gives generously to all without finding fault, and it will be given to you. But when you ask, you must believe and not doubt, because the one who doubts is like a wave of the sea, blown and tossed by the wind. That person should not expect to receive anything from the Lord. Such a person is double-minded and unstable in all they do.*

Consider This

Prayer can mean a lot of things to a lot of people. From the evening news to the football state championship to the cancer wing of the hospital, the word *prayer* gets casually tossed about like a topping of sorts. "We will keep you in our prayers" can be spoken almost as casually as "Can you pass the salt?" In the New Testament, prayer means something infinitely more powerful.

In the New Testament, prayer is a determined and confident clinging to God in the face of challenging circumstances. For the follower of Jesus, prayer is not the last resort but the first response. Prayer is not the last-second Hail Mary pass into the end zone; it is the strategy and substance of the entire game.

> If any of you lacks wisdom, let him ask God, who gives generously to all without reproach, and it will be given him. (ESV)

Prayer opens the doorway into the wisdom of God. Remember, though, New Testament prayer is new. How? Remember how Jesus taught us to pray? "This, then, is how you should pray: 'Our Father in heaven'" (Matthew 6:9). James reiterates this instruction, teaching us to pray "to the Father." My literal Greek translation of James describes the Father this way: "the generously giving God."

Hear Jesus' continued teaching on prayer: "If you, then, though you are evil, know how to give good gifts to your children, how much more will your Father in heaven give good gifts to those who ask him!" (Matthew 7:11).

New Testament prayer asks, seeks, and knocks—all of this is the movement of faith. The person who goes to their neighbor at midnight to ask for help doesn't have just a hopeful *feeling* that the neighbor will help. No, the person *knows* that the neighbor will help, and therefore they will not give up until the neighbor does. This is not a casual "I'll pray about that" approach; it's the unrelenting pursuit of a good Father. (From another angle, consider the widow's persistence in Luke 18:1–8.)

Rather than the common misunderstanding that doubt is the opposite of faith, James will teach us that inaction is faith's nemesis. Doubt is the opposite of prayer. Prayer takes on doubt with determined action, believing in a generously good Father God who will intervene with wisdom, guidance, and aid. Doubt is a given for people. The question is how we will deal with our doubt. Prayer walks us along a path where doubt is transformed into faith.

Prayer is releasing our worry in the presence of God. Prayer means not letting go because God never lets go. Worrying our prayers, says James, is a recipe for complete instability and endless, aimless drifting, being tossed to and fro on the waves. Certainly, we must come to God as we are, worries and all, but we approach with a determination to abandon ourselves to God, which initially means to "cast all your anxiety on him because he cares for you" (1 Peter 5:7).

The timeless wisdom of Proverbs 3:5–6 captures it with precision. In these words lives the very substance and ethos of prayer: "Trust in the Lord with all your heart and lean not on your own understanding; in all your ways submit to him, and he will make your paths straight."

You may be asking, "So we pray and believe, and then what? How do we know we have actually received wisdom from God?" This is the critical question. To believe and not doubt means rising up into a new attentiveness and alertness to the presence of God. It means trusting that the Holy Spirit is infusing our instincts with direction we can count on. It's not a certain feeling or a particular way of hearing God's voice; it's moving in reliance on the generous God who gives and guides us every step of the way—like a divine GPS.

The Prayer

God our Father, I need wisdom, and I need it all the time. Teach me how to pray for wisdom and not to doubt that you will give it to me. In fact, increase my faith to the point of acting on the instincts that my prayer is already being answered. Come, Holy Spirit, and make me bold. In Jesus' name. Amen.

The Questions

How do you relate to the idea of doubt not being the opposite of faith, but rather the opposite of prayer? Do you grasp how prayer is an action strategy to move from doubt to faith? The opposite of faith is inaction. How could this change your approach to certain situations in your life right now where you find yourself stuck?

What would it mean for you to follow your prayer for wisdom with genuine belief that you will be given wisdom? What might it be like to move in faith that God is answering rather than waiting on some particular experience or sign?

How might you make asking God for wisdom a more tangible act rather than a passing thought in your head (as our prayers can often become)? Could you try writing it down? What can make prayer a more defined, tangible action, such that it can be an active confrontation of doubt?

6 James 1:9–12

The Big Problem with First-World Problems

Let the lowly brother boast in his exaltation, and the rich in his humiliation, because like a flower of the grass he will pass away. For the sun rises with its scorching heat and withers the grass; its flower falls, and its beauty perishes. So also will the rich man fade away in the midst of his pursuits.

Blessed is the man who remains steadfast under trial, for when he has stood the test he will receive the crown of life, which God has promised to those who love him. (ESV)

Consider This

As we proceed with James, I want to say a few words about context. James, like the rest of the books in the Bible, was written to a particular group of people dealing with specific real-world problems at a defined time in history. One of the golden rules of interpreting the Bible we must never forget is this: It still means today what it meant to its original hearers. Scripture cannot mean whatever we want it to mean. At the same time, the Bible cannot be limited to a first-century application.

I think of interpretation and application like a circular target with a bull's-eye in the center and concentric surrounding rings. The bull's-eye would be the particular first-century meaning and application. The outer rings would signify a range of acceptable applications throughout the history of the church and to the present day. Outside of the target itself are the range of meanings and applications that cannot be legitimately supported by the text. Today's text illustrates this target well.

James 1:12 revisits the issue of trials and perseverance again as it did in verses 2–4. A good question to ask of the text is, "To which kinds of tests and trials is James referring?" Let's say I'm on trial for a crime for which I am admittedly guilty. Is this the kind of trial James means? In order to determine this, our next question to James might be, "What did you mean when you wrote this, James?" He tells us by means of the context. Verses 9–11 give us a big clue. James is dealing with Christians who face economic oppression and are being treated unjustly—to the point of humiliation—by the rich. This theme is not new to the Bible. Remember Isaiah? How about Amos?

Back to my trial metaphor—does it qualify as one of the kinds of trials I can consider to be "pure joy"? Perhaps the law I broke is an unjust law and one designed to favor the rich at the cost of the poor—that would complicate things. For the sake of the example, let's posit that my crime was garden-variety theft. I have violated one of the Ten Commandments—stealing—and I am in the process of willfully violating another one—bearing false witness. I think this trial misses the target entirely. I am merely facing the consequences of my sinful actions.

Twisting the plot a bit, let's say I didn't do the crime but have been unjustly accused. I can't afford a lawyer, and I'm being prosecuted by my landlord, who wants to evict me from my home on the grounds that I violated the terms of the lease by committing the crime—and all of this because he wants to raise the rent and attract a more economically advantaged tenant. All of a sudden we have a trial that not only qualifies for James but also seems to hit the bull's-eye.

Let's try another example. On your way to deliver food to a few shut-ins, you get hit from behind by a semitruck, which totals your vehicle and puts you in the hospital with permanently debilitating but not life-threatening injuries. Is this outside of the realm of the tests and trials James refers to? It doesn't necessarily involve economic exploitation. At the same time, remember from verse 2 that James mentioned "trials of many kinds." I would say this one misses the bull's-eye but instead hits the target and qualifies as a trial I must endure as a testing of my faith, a trial that can be turned to my good through the persevering work of the Holy Spirit to bring me to completeness and maturity of faith.

Why does this matter? Chances are, if you are reading this, it may never have occurred to you that today's text is all about the upending of the rich and the exaltation of the poor. Chances are, if you're anything like me, you read right over the original context and immediately ran to your own tests and trials, which in all likelihood qualify for the category of first-world problems—challenges not even remotely in the realm of the biblical meaning. For example, your third riverfront home was destroyed by flooding. But look on the bright side, the flood also cleared the shoreline of all those uninsured shacks inhabited by the riffraff you wanted out of there anyway.

Are you feeling the jarring disorientation of this text? That's what James is looking for. It's not so much about my son being on academic probation at college this semester as it is about the millions of orphans around the world who won't be able to go to first grade this year.

While we cannot help but read James as "the rich" (relatively speaking), James insists that we read it with "the poor."

The Prayer

God our Father, open my eyes to understand the difference between a real trial and an inconvenience. Attune my mind and heart to the trials of so many who have so little. Open my eyes to my relative wealth in this world and to the reality of poverty all around me. In Jesus' name. Amen.

The Questions

What, if anything, upsets you about today's reflections on this passage? Why does it upset you? Why doesn't it?

Which tests and trials in your life seem to land in the target James has in mind? Which ones might not?

What about fellow believers who are facing economic injustice or oppression? Are they reaping what they have sown? Or could their disadvantaged situation be beyond their cause or control? What response might we make to them?

Week 1: Discussion Questions

Hearing the Text: Read James 1:1–12

James, a servant of God and of the Lord Jesus Christ,

To the twelve tribes scattered among the nations:

Greetings.

Consider it pure joy, my brothers and sisters, whenever you face trials of many kinds, because you know that the testing of your faith produces perseverance. Let perseverance finish its work so that you may be mature and complete, not lacking anything. If any of you lacks wisdom, you should ask God, who gives generously to all without finding fault, and it will be given to you. But when you ask, you must believe and not doubt, because the one who doubts is like a wave of the sea, blown and tossed by the wind. That person should not expect to receive anything from the Lord. Such a person is double-minded and unstable in all they do.

Believers in humble circumstances ought to take pride in their high position. But the rich should take pride in their humiliation—since they will pass away like a wild flower. For the sun rises with scorching heat and withers the plant; its blossom falls and its beauty is destroyed. In the same way, the rich will fade away even while they go about their business.

Blessed is the one who perseveres under trial because, having stood the test, that person will receive the crown of life that the Lord has promised to those who love him.

Responding to the Text

- What did you hear?
- What did you see?
- What did you otherwise sense from the Lord?

Sharing Insights and Implications for Discipleship

Drawing from the Scripture text and daily readings, what did you find challenging, encouraging, provocative, comforting, invasive, inspiring, corrective, affirming, guiding, or warning?

Shaping Intentions for Prayer

Write your discipleship intention for the week ahead.

2

WEEK

James 1:13–2:7

8

James 1:13–15

Why Pinning Can Lead to Sinning

When tempted, no one should say, "God is tempting me." For God cannot be tempted by evil, nor does he tempt anyone; but each person is tempted when they are dragged away by their own evil desire and enticed. Then, after desire has conceived, it gives birth to sin; and sin, when it is full-grown, gives birth to death.

Consider This

Okay, Pinterest nation, no pin throwing. This post is not against pinning, but rather an effort to help us understand the nature of sinning. How does sin work? According to James, the progression looks something like this: enticement—desire—captivation—conception—sin—growth—death.

We need look no further than the original sin to see the pattern at work:

> So when the woman saw that the tree was good for food [enticement], and that it was a delight to the eyes [desire], and that the tree was to be desired [captivation] to make one wise [conception], she took of its fruit and ate [sin], and she also gave some to her husband who was with her [growth], and he ate [death]. (Genesis 3:6 ESV)

Now, the big problem we have with sin and the reason we so ineffectively deal with it is that we don't seriously engage the problem until it reaches the stage of behavior. We mistakenly think of sin as external behavior when in reality it is an internal disposition.

Didn't Jesus say as much in the Sermon on the Mount about adultery and murder? He identified the internal dispositions of lust and anger as the genesis of the problem.

So what if instead of the futility of trying to manage our behavior, we developed a strategy of disciplining our desires? Until desire comes under the discipline of the Word of God and the Spirit of God, it is inherently untrustworthy and predisposed to evil. As my friend and mentor Timothy Tennent is fond of saying, "Sin must cease to be our secret lover and be clearly identified as our mortal enemy."

Our discipleship must get beneath our legalistic, shame-based orientation with sin as behavior. We must become discerning and unflinchingly honest about our dispositions. What are our particular proclivities toward sin? Where are we most subject to being enticed? Rather than betting the farm on a legalistic "don't look" approach, we must learn the way of delighting ourselves in the Lord. Psalm 37:4 comes to mind: "Delight yourself in the Lord, and he will give you the desires of your heart" (ESV).

Back to Pinterest. Pinning is an exercise in delighting. As I said, it's not a bad thing, until it is. For me, it's a pretty short journey from pinning to one-click ordering. Seriously, instead of knocking the practice of pinning, what if we learned to pin all the ways, means, and reasons for which we might delight ourselves in the Lord?

Hoping we are going to overcome sin, especially those besetting sins that plague us, will never get it done. Hope, as has been famously said, is not a strategy. Sin creates the most sophisticated strategies known to the human race. Left to our own devices, we don't stand a chance. Grace offers a superior strategy, with the capacity to utterly destroy sin in our lives. Why, then, do we keep getting "dragged away," as today's text so graphically puts it?

I've got a theory about that.

We aren't losing the battle against sin for lack of going to church, Bible study, prayer, or even fasting. We are losing because we are trying to go at it alone. We are losing because we haven't trusted another human being with the vulnerable knowledge of our own broken dispositions, sinful proclivities, and otherwise untrained desires. Sin wins in isolation. It doesn't stand a chance against the humble and holy work of brothers and sisters watching over one another in love.

The Prayer

God, our Father, I am so easily distracted and dragged away. Soften my heart to become aware at the first knock of sin and give me the grace not to walk toward but to run away. Attune me to my sin proclivities and propensities, and guide me toward others who can help me conquer these ways that so distract and defeat me. In Jesus' name. Amen.

The Questions

We all sin differently. Have you discovered the deeper dispositions that underlie your particular proclivities to sin? How would you describe them?

Instead of legalistic declarations and self-shaming, what might delighting yourself in the Lord look like as a strategy for the discipleship of desire?

Does sin in general or do certain sins remain for you as a type of affair with a secret lover? Are you ready to declare war on sin, decrying it as the mortal enemy of your soul?

Have you ever trusted another human being with your own dispositional proclivities toward particular sins? Don't feel bad if you have not; very few actually have. Are you ready to consider this possibility?

9

James 1:16–18

The Deception of Self-Deception

Don't be deceived, my dear brothers and sisters. Every good and perfect gift is from above, coming down from the Father of the heavenly lights, who does not change like shifting shadows. He chose to give us birth through the word of truth, that we might be a kind of firstfruits of all he created.

Consider This

Don't be deceived.

The big problem with deception is how deceptive it actually is. A person who is deceived or who is in the process of being deceived has no idea whether it has happened or is happening. Deception's greatest power is its ability to hide itself from its intended victim.

Look at the interchange between God and Eve in Eden after the fateful act of rebellion. "Then the LORD God said to the woman, 'What is this you have done?' The woman said, 'The serpent deceived me, and I ate'" (Genesis 3:13).

Deception works through preying on our undiscipled desires with all manner of enticement. Remember our text from yesterday? "Then, after desire has conceived, it gives birth to sin; and sin, when it is full -grown, gives birth to death" (James 1:15).

Now watch the contrast with today's text:

> He chose to give us birth through the word of truth, that we might be a kind of firstfruits of all he created.

In contrast to the shifting shadows of sin, God is light, and as the apostle John put it, "In him there is no darkness" (1 John 1:5). Instead of deception and desire leading to the birth of sin, our God sovereignly gives birth to his people through his "word of truth." Truth cuts through deception like light cuts through darkness. Sin works through isolating us in our desires. God works to disciple and sanctify our desires through the gifts of his Word, his Spirit, and his people.

So how does one steer clear of deception? To try to suppress or destroy desire is futile. Our desire must be given a better object. We must invite the Holy Spirit to teach and train our desires so that we may delight ourselves in the Lord. The Spirit will always bring us back to the "word of truth" through which God has given us new birth.

Now about this "firstfruits" business. A firstfruits offering is just what it sounds like. It means to bring the first portion of a harvest and offer it to the Lord. A firstfruits offering is a sign of the promise of the rest of the harvest to come. The amazing thing in today's text is the way it reverses the firstfruits offering. We aren't making an offering of firstfruits to God; God is making an offering of firstfruits to the world. The firstfruits of the harvest is not grain; the firstfruits of the harvest is us—those whom he has given birth through the "word of truth." We are God's firstfruits offering to the world. Through us, God is revealing to the world the power of his promise—to bring all who believe in him out of deception and into the light of his truth.

What do you delight in? Where do your desires lead you astray?

The Prayer

God our Father, I want to be like your Son, Jesus, who is the truth. Awaken me to the ways I am susceptible to deception. Come, Holy Spirit, and disciple my desires until I am pure in heart and can see God clearly. In Jesus' name. Amen.

The Questions

Is it possible that you could be deceived about some area of sin in your life?

If you responded to the preceding question with no, then you are likely at risk of being deceived in some area of your life. Consider this word from the prophet Jeremiah: "The heart is deceitful above all things and beyond cure. Who can understand it? 'I the LORD search the heart and examine the mind, to reward each person according to their conduct, according to what their deeds deserve'" (17:9–10).

Is it possible that you could be deceived about some area of sin in your life? What would it look like for you to open your heart to the gracious searching of the Holy Spirit? Try this prayer: "Search me, God, and know my heart; test me and know my anxious thoughts. See if there is any offensive way in me, and lead me in the way everlasting" (Psalm 139:23–24).

10 James 1:19–21

A Strategy Beyond Anger Management

> *My dear brothers and sisters, take note of this: Everyone should be quick to listen, slow to speak and slow to become angry, because human anger does not produce the righteousness that God desires. Therefore, get rid of all moral filth and the evil that is so prevalent and humbly accept the word planted in you, which can save you.*

Consider This

A few verses back, James sternly warned us, "Don't be deceived" (1:16). Though he seems to shift gears quickly to talk about anger, we can't so quickly leave the problem of deception behind. So what do anger and deception have to do with one another? While anger can be a justified response to being wronged, it readily leads one to return the favor —answering a wrong with a wrong. Justified anger feels so right and powerful that it can be intoxicating. In this state, one can be easily deceived that this anger is a righteous anger and warrants a decisive response.

Master Yoda's response to the young Anakin Skywalker in the *Star Wars* saga is instructive. "Fear is the path to the dark side. Fear leads to anger. Anger leads to hate. Hate leads to suffering."[1]

Perhaps the biggest temptation in the midst of a difficult test or trial, especially if it involves some form of injustice or oppression, is to fight back in anger. James is giving us a very practical strategy: Be quick to listen, slow to speak, slow to become angry.

I'm not sure if it's still the case, but it used to be that a car or truck had warning light gauges on the dashboard. With a gauge, we are able to keep an eye on something—for example, a motor that is running

1. "Master Yoda Quote (FEAR), Star Wars I—The Phantom Menace (1999)," www.youtube.com/watch?v=91_G8iaokk8.

hot. We can make adjustments. Without gauges, we are left with a red light; and when it comes on, it's too late. The engine has already boiled over. People are like that. Anger has a way of sneaking up on us. We don't see it coming, and by the time it is upon us, it's too late. We have already boiled over. Are you attuned to your anger quotient? Do you have a gauge? Anger is not itself a bad thing; it's what we do with the anger that matters. Will we develop the ability to see it coming so we can slow down our response and perhaps counteract it with more focused listening in the midst of a hot situation?

It matters "because human anger does not produce the righteousness that God desires." Anger produces self-righteousness. It is all too often the expression of a wounded pride. Our anger should remind us of a truth about God—he is slow to anger and abounding in love.

> Therefore, get rid of all moral filth and the evil that is so prevalent and humbly accept the word planted in you, which can save you.

I love how Eugene Peterson translates this in *The Message*: "In simple humility, let our gardener, God, landscape you with the Word, making a salvation-garden of your life."

Anger works like a weed. Weeds take an inordinate amount of water and nutrients from the soil. Weeds grow fast, quickly reproduce, and grow out of control. Weeds bear no fruit. And worst of all, weeds choke the life out of the healthy fruit-bearing plants around them. Yep, that's exactly what anger does. The Word of God not only gives us life, but it cultivates growth and fruitfulness in our lives. I want God to landscape me with the Word planted in me, making a salvation-garden of my life. I want that for you too.

The Prayer

God our Father, landscape me with your Word and make a salvation-garden of my life. I want to be rid of the filth and evil that so deeply impacts and infects me. Come, Holy Spirit, help me humbly accept the Word planted in me, which can save me. In Jesus' name. Amen.

The Questions

What about your anger quotient? Are you quick to get angry at what can seemingly be a small thing—like someone cutting you off in traffic? Ask yourself this question: "What am I really mad about?"

Can you think of someone in your past or present life who is "quick to listen"? Be on the lookout for that. What can you learn from them?

What about being "slow to speak"? Take an audit of your speech today and pay attention to how many times you quickly begin talking to justify yourself, something you did, or your position or argument in a given situation. How much of your speech is self-justifying? The answer may surprise you. Self-righteousness is, in essence, the insatiable need to be right, and a person who always needs to be right most often has anger seething just under the surface.

Finally, what could it look like for the Holy Spirit to become your landscaper, landscaping you with the Word planted in you in order to make a marvelous garden space of your inner (and outer) life? What would it mean for you to move in this direction "in simple humility," as the text instructs?

11

James 1:22–25

The Age of the Selfie on Steroids

Do not merely listen to the word, and so deceive yourselves. Do what it says. Anyone who listens to the word but does not do what it says is like someone who looks at his face in a mirror and, after looking at himself, goes away and immediately forgets what he looks like. But whoever looks intently into the perfect law that gives freedom, and continues in it—not forgetting what they have heard, but doing it—they will be blessed in what they do.

Consider This

One of my favorite lines from the movie *Forrest Gump* comes to mind in response to today's text: "Stupid is as stupid does."[2]

James is moving us to a place where a variation of Gump's quote seems apropos: "Faith is as faith does."

Unless faith moves, it cannot be called faith. We live in the age of easy believism, where we are quite willing to satisfy ourselves with a mental assent to a stated proposition. Do you believe that Jesus died for your sins? Answer yes, and you get a check in the box next to faith. James calls this kind of approach *self-deception*.

> Do not merely listen to the word, and so deceive yourselves. Do what it says.

Let's take it a step further. Reading the Bible, praying, fasting, and other exercises of Christian devotion cannot be mistaken for the activity of faith. These are ways of looking "intently into the perfect law that gives freedom" and can be helpful in the ongoing process of continuing to do so, aiding us in "not forgetting." But unless all of it leads to the action of faith, it will amount to nothing.

Consider this example: One of the toys we gave our youngest child came with those three most dreadful words of Christmas: Some assembly required. Imagine that Sam and I had read through those instructions each day, talked about them together, looked intently at all of the dislocated parts and pieces in the box, and left it at that. Do you think Sam would be okay with that approach? Now imagine we spent hours assembling it, after which Sam promptly put it on the shelf and never touched it again. We would have gone through all the motions but never moved on to the action of using the toy.

So much of the so-called Christian faith these days is just that—a faithfulness to read the instructions, assent to the truth of it all, commit the instructions to memory, get together in groups to study the instructions, and maybe even go to a conference with a lot of other people

2. "Can You Complete These Forrest Gump Quotes?!" (Paramount Movies, 1994), www.youtube.com/shorts/DZ4WDy0OIYQ.

committed to the instructions, but to never put anything together that goes anywhere. Motions can keep us moving endlessly yet still not see us making any significant movement. There's a lot of activity but in the end no real action. Don't hear me wrong, the motions and the activity are important, but unless they are leading to the active doing of the subject matter being intently focused on, it's a waste of time.

> Anyone who listens to the word but does not do what it says is like someone who looks at his face in a mirror and, after looking at himself, goes away and immediately forgets what he looks like.

One of the most bizarre practices of our time is the act of standing in front of a mirror while looking at yourself in the mirror and taking a photo of the mirror in which you are looking at yourself. It's like a selfie on steroids. I'm not even sure how to think about that other than to say I think James would have a field day with the metaphor. In some ways, it captures the spirit of our age and the religious enterprise of endless devotional activity we have come to equate with the Christian faith.

> But whoever looks intently into the perfect law that gives freedom, and continues in it—not forgetting what they have heard, but doing it—they will be blessed in what they do.

Be clear. Let's not deceive ourselves by creating a false choice between, for example, reading Scripture and taking care of people in need. We must look intently into the perfect law and continue in it, determined to not forget what we have heard. We must do it.

The Prayer

God our Father, I want to be a real Christian. Lead me from being a reader of your Word to becoming a doer of it. Let me not be deceived into believing my daily devotions are my doings. Make them rather a springboard into the actions of faith and all for your glory. In Jesus' name. Amen.

The Questions

What do you make of this notion of religious motions but no faith movement? Can you see evidence of this phenomenon in your past? Your present?

While a person's devotional life fuels their faith, it cannot be mistaken for the actual action that faith requires. Do you agree or disagree with this statement, and why?

What would it look like for you to make a commitment to never walk away from hearing the Word of God again without some tangible action that you could do going forward?

What might that mean from today's reading?

12

James 1:26–27

The Way True Religion Breaks the Self-Deception of False Faith

> *Those who consider themselves religious and yet do not keep a tight rein on their tongues deceive themselves, and their religion is worthless. Religion that God our Father accepts as pure and faultless is this: to look after orphans and widows in their distress and to keep oneself from being polluted by the world.*

Consider This

James just can't leave this business of deception behind.

In 1:16, he warned, "Don't be deceived, my dear brothers and sisters."

In 1:22, he warned again, "Do not merely listen to the word, and so deceive yourselves."

Now today he says it again in verse 26:

> If anyone thinks he is religious and does not bridle his tongue but deceives his heart, this person's religion is worthless. (ESV)

Chances are no one reading this book (or the one writing it) actually thinks they are being deceived. That's how deception works. We don't know it when it's happening. So what are we to do? Should we go around being suspicious of everyone and wary of being tricked? No. The danger is not from other people; it is from ourselves. The issue is self-deception.

Anyone who has lived any amount of time knows that a human person has an almost infinite capacity to deceive themselves. It's why people cheat on their taxes and steal from their employers. It's how people rationalize extramarital affairs. It's how preachers find their way into pornography. It's why many people in prison today consider themselves innocent. When it comes to self-deception, there are infinite shades of gray. In all of these situations, people manage to talk a good game when it comes to religious faith.

Back in 1:21, James gave us a helpful admonition: "Therefore, get rid of all moral filth and the evil that is so prevalent and humbly accept the word planted in you, which can save you."

Look at the seemingly disconnected admonition he offers today:

> Religion that God our Father accepts as pure and faultless is this: to look after orphans and widows in their distress and to keep oneself from being polluted by the world.

What does looking after widows and orphans have to do with overcoming self-deception? Maybe it has something to do with our inability to think, read, or pray our way out of the grip of self-deception. Could it be that self-deception can only be broken by the sobering activity of selfless giving? What if true religion is the only way out of false faith? The crazy thing about impure and faulty religion is that people can hold all the right beliefs and maintain all the right religious motions, yet still be steeped in false faith.

I mostly see change happen when Christians go on a mission trip.

They find themselves in an orphanage somewhere south of the equator, far from the comforts of suburban seductions and small-town distractions. An inescapable confrontation begins to happen. Their hearts begin to break over the kind of human need and suffering that breaks the heart of God. A kind of awakening begins to happen. True religion, in the way James identifies it, has a way of exposing the self-deceiving ways of false religion like nothing else can.

The Prayer

God our Father, I want to be a real Christian. I don't think I am deceived, which is likely a good sign that I am. Break the deception in me. Show me the path toward true religion, which is my selfless giving to those who need it the most. Break me out of the hall of mirrors that my life so easily becomes. In Jesus' name. Amen.

The Questions

According to today's text, we don't keep ourselves "from being polluted by the world" by escaping the world. It happens as we enter into the broken world in a different way. Does this make sense to you? How?

Have you had an experience of practicing true religion as James describes it? Did it open your eyes to see the world and faith differently? How? Can you think of a person whose life and faith were transformed by helping others in need?

How does looking after orphans and widows in their distress break through the smoke screen of self-deceived religion? What does it expose about our churches, our own faith, and our values?

13

James 2:1–7

The Way We Treat "the Help"

My brothers and sisters, believers in our glorious Lord Jesus Christ must not show favoritism. Suppose a man comes into your meeting wearing a gold ring and fine clothes, and a poor man in filthy old clothes also comes in. If you show special attention to the man wearing fine clothes and say, "Here's a good seat for you," but say to the poor man, "You stand there" or "Sit on the floor by my feet," have you not discriminated among yourselves and become judges with evil thoughts?

Listen, my dear brothers and sisters: Has not God chosen those who are poor in the eyes of the world to be rich in faith and to inherit the kingdom he promised those who love him? But you have dishonored the poor. Is it not the rich who are exploiting you? Are they not the ones who are dragging you into court? Are they not the ones who are blaspheming the noble name of him to whom you belong?

Consider This

I am not a famous person, nor am I widely known, but I am well-known in some circles. It's fascinating when I find myself in a setting where a lot of people know me. I am treated with honor and respect, and many people will want to talk with me. More often than not, though, I find myself in situations where I am virtually unknown. No one seeks me out for conversation. People don't care much about meeting me or interacting with me. I am the same person in both situations, yet I am treated quite differently.

We all do it. We pay more attention to the people who tend to increase our status and importance, or who could do something for us. We pay less attention to the people who can't help us, who lack the importance, wealth, or wherewithal to do anything for us.

You find out the most about a person by the way they treat other people who they perceive can't do anything for them. Observe how people treat waiters in restaurants. If you are with a person and they are unkind to the waiter, chances are they aren't a very good person. The way we treat "the help" says a lot more about us than it does about "the help."

Why didn't God come to us as a rich person? God could have been born into any family in the entire world. Why did he choose to be born into a poor family? Why did God choose to come to us as a person without influence, power, or fame?

Have you ever asked yourself these questions?

> My brothers and sisters, believers in our glorious Lord Jesus Christ must not show favoritism.

When God became a person, he chose to become a nobody. If there is anything we can learn from this, it would seem to be the importance of treating those we perceive as nobodies as though they were somebody, and handling people we consider unimportant as especially important. It's especially fascinating when we consider the way Jesus framed the final judgment.

> Then the King will say to those on his right, "Come, you who are blessed by my Father; take your inheritance, the kingdom prepared for you since the creation of the world. For I was hungry and you gave me something to eat, I was thirsty and you gave me something to drink, I was a stranger and you invited me in, I needed clothes and you clothed me, I was sick and you looked after me, I was in prison and you came to visit me." (Matthew 25:34–36)

Let's leave it there today.

The Prayer

God our Father, I want to be a real Christian. Reveal to me how self-interested I am in the way I treat other people. Expose the ways I show favoritism in order to benefit myself. Open my eyes and my heart to the people I perceive can do nothing for me and teach me to love them. In Jesus' name. Amen.

The Questions

What is it about us that makes us want to be connected to important people?

Do you ever find yourself wanting to let other people know of your importance, accomplishments, or the important people you know?

Do you treat wealthy people differently from the way you treat poor people? What practical steps can you take today to change this approach?

Week 2: Discussion Questions

Hearing the Text: Read James 1:13–2:7

When tempted, no one should say, "God is tempting me." For God cannot be tempted by evil, nor does he tempt anyone; but each person is tempted when they are dragged away by their own evil desire and enticed. Then, after desire has conceived, it gives birth to sin; and sin, when it is full-grown, gives birth to death.

Don't be deceived, my dear brothers and sisters. Every good and perfect gift is from above, coming down from the Father of the heavenly lights, who does not change like shifting shadows. He chose to give us birth through the word of truth, that we might be a kind of firstfruits of all he created.

My dear brothers and sisters, take note of this: Everyone should be quick to listen, slow to speak and slow to become angry, because human anger does not produce the righteousness that God desires. Therefore, get rid of all moral filth and the evil that is so prevalent and humbly accept the word planted in you, which can save you.

Do not merely listen to the word, and so deceive yourselves. Do what it says. Anyone who listens to the word but does not do what it says is like someone who looks at his face in a mirror and, after looking at himself, goes away and immediately forgets what he looks like. But whoever looks intently into the perfect law that gives freedom, and continues in it—not forgetting what they have heard, but doing it—they will be blessed in what they do.

Those who consider themselves religious and yet do not keep a tight rein on their tongues deceive themselves, and their religion is worthless. Religion that God our Father accepts as pure and faultless is this: to look after orphans and widows in their distress and to keep oneself from being polluted by the world.

My brothers and sisters, believers in our glorious Lord Jesus Christ must not show favoritism. Suppose a man comes into your meeting wearing a gold ring and fine clothes, and a poor man in filthy old clothes also comes in. If you show special attention to the man wearing fine clothes and say, "Here's a good seat for you," but say to the poor man, "You stand there" or "Sit on the floor by my feet," have you not discriminated among yourselves and become judges with evil thoughts?

Listen, my dear brothers and sisters: Has not God chosen those who are poor in the eyes of the world to be rich in faith and to inherit the kingdom he promised those who love him? But you have dishonored the poor. Is it not the rich who are exploiting you? Are they not the ones who are dragging you into court? Are they not the ones who are blaspheming the noble name of him to whom you belong?

Responding to the Text

- What did you hear?
- What did you see?
- What did you otherwise sense from the Lord?

Sharing Insights and Implications for Discipleship

Drawing from the Scripture text and daily readings, what did you find challenging, encouraging, provocative, comforting, invasive, inspiring, corrective, affirming, guiding, or warning?

Shaping Intentions for Prayer

Write your discipleship intention for the week ahead.

3
WEEK

James 2:8–3:8

15

James 2:8–13

How to Know If You Really Love God

> *If you really keep the royal law found in Scripture, "Love your neighbor as yourself," you are doing right. But if you show favoritism, you sin and are convicted by the law as lawbreakers. For whoever keeps the whole law and yet stumbles at just one point is guilty of breaking all of it. For he who said, "You shall not commit adultery," also said, "You shall not murder." If you do not commit adultery but do commit murder, you have become a lawbreaker.*
>
> *Speak and act as those who are going to be judged by the law that gives freedom, because judgment without mercy will be shown to anyone who has not been merciful. Mercy triumphs over judgment.*

Consider This

What is the royal law of Scripture?

If someone asked me that question, I would likely answer, "Love the Lord your God with all your heart, soul, mind, and strength," or something to that effect. That's not how James sees it.

> If you really keep the royal law found in Scripture, "Love your neighbor as yourself," you are doing right.

James doesn't cite loving God as the supreme law of Scripture. In other words, it's not whether or not we say we love God or how much religious devotion we can demonstrate in support of our love for God. James always makes us put our money where our mouths are. He wants to see the proof. When we boil love for God down to its core, it always comes back to loving people. If a person claims to love God but does not love people, their claim is empty. They are self-deceived.

We typically interpret the law with reference to ourselves. It's all about what we are forbidden to do—what is against the law. We can say we have kept the law by identifying what we have elected not to do. James wants us to shift gears into thinking of the law with reference to other people—who the law is for. In other words, the royal law of Scripture is love. Law is not about restriction; law is about love. We should not think of the law in terms of whether we have broken it, but in terms of whether we have injured, harmed, or wrecked another person. This is how Jesus is able to summarize his rule in a single command: "My command is this: Love each other as I have loved you" (John 15:12). If our lives are oriented around the royal law of love, which means we are progressively free from our own selfishness, we need not be concerned about breaking any laws. Love is both the freedom and the fulfillment of the law. Far from legalistic perfection, righteousness—in the vision of God—means perfect love for other people. Loving others is the definitive sign that a person loves God.

> Speak and act as those who are going to be judged by the law that gives freedom, because judgment without mercy will be shown to anyone who has not been merciful. Mercy triumphs over judgment.

The law that gives freedom is the royal law of love. Love's first impulse is the movement to show mercy. It is human nature to want to make judgments against people and to seek justice. The nature of God is to make judgments and to show mercy. Mercy is not the absence of judgment, but the triumph over it. Merciful people aren't soft on crime; they see a bigger picture. Merciful people, above all, profoundly understand their own need for mercy. They are no longer self-deceived about their own righteousness. They have seen a bigger God.

The Prayer

God our Father, I want to be a real Christian. Teach me the truth that I cannot love you apart from loving other people and that I cannot truly love them apart from loving you. Even more, train me in your mercy to love like you love. In Jesus' name. Amen.

The Questions

What would it mean to switch your perspective from trying not to break the law to walking in the obedience of love? Do you see how it changes your point of reference from yourself to other people?

Are you a merciful person? Or do you tend to think people should get what's coming to them? Do you err on the side of mercy or judgment? What will it take for you to err on the side of mercy?

What if you began to see sin not as the breaking of a rule but as the failure of love? How would that change your way of life?

16

James 2:14–19

Why Mere Belief Won't Get It Done

What good is it, my brothers and sisters, if someone claims to have faith but has no deeds? Can such faith save them? Suppose a brother or a sister is without clothes and daily food. If one of you says to them, "Go in peace; keep warm and well fed," but does nothing about their physical needs, what good is it? In the same way, faith by itself, if it is not accompanied by action, is dead.

But someone will say, "You have faith; I have deeds."

Show me your faith without deeds, and I will show you my faith by my deeds. You believe that there is one God. Good! Even the demons believe that—and shudder.

Consider This

James has led up to this point in his letter with a series of jabs. He has let us know his intentions to challenge our faith multiple times. Finally, today, he gives us the right hook. He comes right out into the open and says it. For effect, permit me a one-line paraphrase: *If you say you believe in God and there's nothing in your actions that prove it, you are deceived.*

I often turn to Eugene Peterson's *The Message* to see how he renders such texts as this one:

> Dear friends, do you think you'll get anywhere in this if you learn all the right words but never do anything? Does merely talking about faith indicate that a person really has it? For instance, you come upon an old friend dressed in rags and half-starved and say, "Good morning, friend! Be clothed in Christ! Be filled with the Holy Spirit!" and walk off without providing so much as a coat or a cup of soup—where does that get you? Isn't it obvious that God-talk without God-acts is outrageous nonsense?

How long will we mistakenly equate faith with believing the right things about God? A demon, James says, believes the right things about God yet has no faith in God. When will we stop assuring people that their right beliefs about God constitute saving faith? Faith that cannot be seen in tangible action cannot be called biblical faith. Let's consult the great chapter on faith in Hebrews 11. It begins with these words: "Now faith is confidence in what we hope for and assurance about what we do not see."

Faith is not something that exists in one's head. It lives in one's everyday, walking-around life, or it does not live at all. Faith is the tangible action that produces the visible evidence that what was heretofore invisible can now be seen.

For James, even this level of teaching about faith and deeds is too conceptual. He brings it home with an everyday example: "Suppose a brother or a sister is without clothes and daily food. If one of you says to them, 'Go in peace; keep warm and well fed,' but does nothing about their physical needs, what good is it?"

I think it may be a good idea to stop talking now and just sit with these words from James. Unless there is an end to our words, our actions will never catch up.

The Prayer

God our Father, I want to be a real Christian. Grace me with a faith that proves itself through love—the real live activity of love for other people. Break through my deception with the grace of your truth. In Jesus' name. Amen.

The Questions

Try doing a faith audit on yesterday. Can you think back through your day and remember any points of tangible action that signified your faith in Jesus Christ?

If not yesterday, how far back do you need to go?

Right beliefs about God are good, but they alone do not rise to the level of faith. How does this challenge your notion of saving faith (that is, believing the right things equals salvation)?

If we believe one must *do* the right things in order to be saved and not merely *believe* the right things, how is this not some kind of works-based salvation? Can you articulate the nuance here?

17

James 2:20–26

Put Me In, Coach. I'm Ready to Play Today!

> *You foolish person, do you want evidence that faith without deeds is useless? Was not our father Abraham considered righteous for what he did when he offered his son Isaac on the altar? You see that his faith and his actions were working together, and his faith was made complete by what he did. And the scripture was fulfilled that says,*

"Abraham believed God, and it was credited to him as righteousness," and he was called God's friend. You see that a person is considered righteous by what they do and not by faith alone.

In the same way, was not even Rahab the prostitute considered righteous for what she did when she gave lodging to the spies and sent them off in a different direction? As the body without the spirit is dead, so faith without deeds is dead.

Consider This

How in the world do we know anything about Abraham? Was it because of what he believed about God? Sort of. But how do we know what he believed about God? Yes, we know it because of what he did. Abraham obeyed God. The only reason we have any idea of who Abraham was is because of what Abraham did. I have often wondered how many people God tried to put in the game before Abraham. Many of them probably believed the right things. They probably had better résumés. But when it came down to putting their money where their mouths were, they balked. I can almost hear the echo from heaven: "Next!"

This is why, in the end, it always appears that God chooses the unlikely to accomplish the impossible. Faith means street-level obedience. "Whom shall I send? And who will go for us?" (Isaiah 6:8). The Bible gives the impression that God doesn't care too much about one's past, track record, résumé, or qualifications. God looks for someone, anyone, whose yes is more than a word. The so-called righteousness that comes from the faithfulness of going through the religious motions seems to have little to do with the righteousness that comes from simple obedient action.

Look who James calls as his next witness: "And in the same way was not also Rahab the prostitute justified by works when she received the messengers and sent them out by another way?" (ESV). Think about that for a minute—a righteous prostitute. Wouldn't the conventional church consider that to be an oxymoron on steroids? What this tells me is that anyone can get in the game at any time, regardless of past performance, lack of biblical knowledge, church attendance records, moral perfection or imperfection, eye-popping skills, good teeth, and so forth. All it takes is a willingness to pony up a little obedience, get out on the field, and start playing.

In the end, it's not the people with the most money, the best ideas, or the highest biblical IQ who get honorable mention in the kingdom of God; it's the ones who took the risk of action. That's what faith is all about.

So how about it? Are you ready to say, "Put me in, Coach. I'm ready to play today!"

The Prayer

God our Father, I want to be a real Christian. I want my word to be more than my word; I want my word to be backed up with action. Come, Holy Spirit, and make me a person of action. In Jesus' name. Amen.

The Questions

In what ways have you considered yourself inadequate or unqualified to really play a position on the field of faith?

Is there some failure in your past or brokenness that you think disqualifies you from getting into the game? What will it take to get past this? What would Rahab say to you about that?

What are your excuses for not stepping up to the plate and swinging for the fence of faith? Will these be satisfying reasons for staying on the sideline in the end?

18

James 3:1–2

On Owning Your Life

> *Not many of you should become teachers, my fellow believers, because you know that we who teach will be judged more strictly. We all*

> *stumble in many ways. Anyone who is never at fault in what they say is perfect, able to keep their whole body in check.*

Consider This

Many have assumed that James, like other New Testament writers, is concerned with heretical or false teaching. Given the nature of the rest of his letter and the lack of contextual clues that point to this interpretation, it is probably safe to assume that while James would have been as troubled as the next leader about false teaching, it was not his concern when he said this: "Not many of you should become teachers, my fellow believers, because you know that we who teach will be judged more strictly."

James is lowering the boom here against teachers who aren't measuring up to their own teaching—in other words, teachers who say one thing and do another. Those of us whose lives are a living denial of our message are a far greater threat to the church than heretical teachers. Don't hear me wrong, false teaching holds grave consequences for the church, but hypocritical leaders are a far more common and insidious threat.

Those of us who would be leaders in the Christian movement must come to grips with the fact that we are held to a higher standard. We will be judged more strictly. It scares me, and I suppose that's exactly what James intended. Here's how I interpret his message to me personally:

> John David, you hold tremendous authority—not in and of yourself, but by virtue of the sacred trust others place in you. As a result, you have an enormous responsibility. If you are going to handle the Holy Word of God and not be a doer of this Word, you should probably step down from your position, your role, as a leader of God's people. John David, you are a flawed human being. You will make mistakes, and you will miss the mark at times. We all stumble in many ways. The bottom line is this: Unless and until you have a 100 percent commitment to become the kind of disciple you aspire to make of others, you aren't ready. And I hate to be blunt about it, but you either need to get ready or you need to do something else with your life.

James is *not* saying we have to be a perfect exemplar to lead other people in Christian discipleship. I think he's saying you must be a person who owns their life. Maturity does not mean sinless perfection; it means the shredding of our self-deception through brutal honesty with ourselves and the humility to own our failures and repent from our mistakes. It requires the absolute abandonment of pretension and a gentle accountability to a few other people who are committed to seeing you become your truest self, which is what it means to truly be Christlike.

Too many leaders (and Christians in general) make the well-intentioned mistake of saying things like, "I'm a sinner just like you." It so easily becomes a way of affirming each other in our arrested development. It produces a profoundly laissez-faire discipleship. The better approach is to say, "I'm a human being just like you. My humanity has been badly deformed by sin, but I'm determined to become a more real, true, loving, alive, and free human being—the kind of human being God intended when he imaged me with his own glory. And by the truth of the Word of God, the power of the Holy Spirit who lives in me, and your grace, I will get there. I want you to come with me."

The Prayer

God our Father, I want to be a real Christian. I confess I am most apt to be deceived when it comes to properly seeing myself. Break through my blindness to my own sin patterns. I cannot confess what I am not aware of. Give me the gift of self-awareness. And draw others to me who will love me enough to tell me the truth. In Jesus' name. Amen.

The Questions

Have you ever encountered a teacher or leader who did not hold themselves to a higher standard?

What do you remember about that situation?

Are you caught or have you ever been caught in a laissez-faire approach to discipleship? For example, "I'm a sinner and that's all I'll ever be, but I'm forgiven and everything will be okay."

On a scale from 1 to 10, with 10 being "in it to win it," where do you rate yourself on the scale of "my life matches my faith"? What can you do to move to the next number up the scale?

19

James 3:3–6

Watch Your Mouth!

> *When we put bits into the mouths of horses to make them obey us, we can turn the whole animal. Or take ships as an example. Although they are so large and are driven by strong winds, they are steered by a very small rudder wherever the pilot wants to go. Likewise, the tongue is a small part of the body, but it makes great boasts. Consider what a great forest is set on fire by a small spark. The tongue also is a fire, a world of evil among the parts of the body. It corrupts the whole body, sets the whole course of one's life on fire, and is itself set on fire by hell.*

Consider This

Up to this point, James has seemed to say that actions speak louder than words. Now he changes gears and points to the power of words. There's a big Bible idea at work when it comes to words. Words create worlds, and words can destroy them. In the beginning, the words of God created the world. Jesus is known as the Word made flesh. And the words of Jesus effected all manner of miracles and blessings (as well as a few choice curses) on our race.

Wisdom comes to us in words. Consider these proverbs:

> The tongue of the righteous is choice silver,
> but the heart of the wicked is of little value.
> The lips of the righteous nourish many,
> but fools die for lack of sense. . . .
> From the mouth of the righteous comes the fruit of wisdom,

but a perverse tongue will be silenced.
The lips of the righteous know what finds favor,
but the mouth of the wicked only what is perverse.
(Proverbs 10:20–21, 31–32)

With their mouths the godless destroy their neighbors,
but through knowledge the righteous escape.
When the righteous prosper, the city rejoices;
when the wicked perish, there are shouts of joy.
Through the blessing of the upright a city is exalted,
but by the mouth of the wicked it is destroyed.
Whoever derides their neighbor has no sense,
but the one who has understanding holds their tongue. (Proverbs 11:9–12)

Words create worlds, and words can destroy them. Our words lead our way, James wisely instructs.

> When we put bits into the mouths of horses to make them obey us, we can turn the whole animal. Or take ships as an example. Although they are so large and are driven by strong winds, they are steered by a very small rudder wherever the pilot wants to go.

"Watch your tongue" is perhaps one of the most apt warnings we can be given.

All of these teachings raise the stakes on God's Word. Nothing could be more important than our immersion in the Word of God, which is our wisdom:

Your word is a lamp for my feet,
a light on my path. . . .
The unfolding of your words gives light;
it gives understanding to the simple. (Psalm 119:105, 130)

More on this in the next chapter.

The Prayer

God our Father, I want to be a real Christian. I can be so casual and callous with my words. Awaken me to the power of my words, and grant me the grace of restraint to withhold harshness. Train my words to speak truth in love, but even more to bless others with the power of your Word. In Jesus' name. Amen.

The Questions

Think back through the past few weeks. Can you remember occasions when someone's words hurt you or brought you down? How about when someone's words built you up or encouraged you? How can words be so powerful?

How about your own words? Remember back over the past day or so. Do an audit on your words. What percentage of your words were destructive? What percentage were constructive and upbuilding?

A lot of people vastly underestimate the power of their words. How about you? Have you come to grips with the power of your words and the impact they have on others?

20

James 3:7–8

On Sticks, Stones, and Words

All kinds of animals, birds, reptiles and sea creatures are being tamed and have been tamed by mankind, but no human being can tame the tongue. It is a restless evil, full of deadly poison.

Consider This

Everyone has heard and remembers the childhood adage, "Sticks and stones can break my bones, but words can never hurt me." It's a lie.

James puts it poignantly: "But no human being can tame the tongue. It is a restless evil, full of deadly poison."

Indeed, our words have the power to build up or to destroy. According to the Bible, our words may be the most powerful thing we have.

Hear these words from the book of Proverbs:

> From the fruit of their lips people are filled with good things,
> and the work of their hands brings them reward. . . .
> The words of the reckless pierce like swords,
> but the tongue of the wise brings healing.
> Truthful lips endure forever,
> but a lying tongue lasts only a moment.
> (Proverbs 12:14, 18–19)

> Gracious words are a honeycomb,
> sweet to the soul and healing to the bones. (Proverbs 16:24)

> The words of the mouth are deep waters,
> but the fountain of wisdom is a rushing stream. . . .
> The tongue has the power of life and death,
> and those who love it will eat its fruit. (Proverbs 18:4, 21)

> Like apples of gold in settings of silver
> is a ruling rightly given. (Proverbs 25:11)

I am fond of asking others, particularly friends, "Do you have a word for me?" My expectation is they will give me one of two possible words—either a word from God for me, or a word of God to me. In other words, a word of prophecy or a word of wisdom. Or if neither of these, then a word from Scripture:

> All kinds of animals, birds, reptiles and sea creatures are being tamed and have been tamed by mankind, but no human being can tame the tongue.

"No human being can tame the tongue." The good news is that the tongue *can* be tamed; we just can't do it on our own. The tongue can be tamed as it is trained by the Word of God and the Spirit of God. It's a crucial aspect of our discipleship to Jesus. Always remember, one of the greatest powers you have resides in your tongue. Use it boldly and yet with great care.

The Prayer

God our Father, I want to be a real Christian. I want my words to reflect your Word and to be inspired and empowered by your Spirit. Awaken me to the power of my tongue. Train my tongue to be a source of great blessing for you and others. In Jesus' name. Amen.

The Questions

Can you remember the last time you intentionally built someone up with your words—not words of flattery but of truth? How did that impact you? How about the person you talked with?

Remember a time when someone's words hurt or wounded you. First, have you forgiven them? What would it look like to become a person who does not return curse for curse, but rather blessing for curse?

Are you coming to grips with the power of your words? How will you grow in the days ahead as a person who blesses others with words? How about today?

Week 3: Discussion Questions

Hearing the Text: Read James 2:8–3:8

If you really keep the royal law found in Scripture, "Love your neighbor as yourself," you are doing right. But if you show favoritism, you sin and are convicted by the law as lawbreakers. For whoever keeps the whole law and yet stumbles at just one point is guilty of breaking all of it. For he who said, "You shall not commit adultery," also said, "You shall not murder." If you do not commit adultery but do commit murder, you have become a lawbreaker.

Speak and act as those who are going to be judged by the law that gives freedom, because judgment without mercy will be shown to anyone who has not been merciful. Mercy triumphs over judgment.

What good is it, my brothers and sisters, if someone claims to have faith but has no deeds? Can such faith save them? Suppose a brother or a sister is without clothes and daily food. If one of you says to them, "Go in peace; keep warm and well fed," but does nothing about their physical needs, what good is it? In the same way, faith by itself, if it is not accompanied by action, is dead.

But someone will say, "You have faith; I have deeds."

Show me your faith without deeds, and I will show you my faith by my deeds. You believe that there is one God. Good! Even the demons believe that—and shudder.

You foolish person, do you want evidence that faith without deeds is useless? Was not our father Abraham considered righteous for what he did when he offered his son Isaac on the altar? You see that his faith and his actions were working together, and his faith was made complete by what he did. And the scripture was fulfilled that says, "Abraham believed God, and it was credited to him as righteousness," and he was called God's friend. You see that a person is considered righteous by what they do and not by faith alone.

In the same way, was not even Rahab the prostitute considered righteous for what she did when she gave lodging to the spies and sent them off in a different direction? As the body without the spirit is dead, so faith without deeds is dead.

Not many of you should become teachers, my fellow believers, because you know that we who teach will be judged more strictly. We all stumble in many ways. Anyone who is never at fault in what they say is perfect, able to keep their whole body in check.

When we put bits into the mouths of horses to make them obey us, we can turn the whole animal. Or take ships as an example. Although they are so large and are driven by strong winds, they are steered by a very small rudder wherever the pilot wants to go. Likewise, the tongue is a small part of the body, but it makes great boasts. Consider what a great forest is set on fire by a small spark. The tongue also is a fire, a world of evil among the parts of the body. It corrupts the whole body, sets the whole course of one's life on fire, and is itself set on fire by hell.

All kinds of animals, birds, reptiles and sea creatures are being tamed and have been tamed by mankind, but no human being can tame the tongue. It is a restless evil, full of deadly poison.

Responding to the Text

- What did you hear?
- What did you see?
- What did you otherwise sense from the Lord?

Sharing Insights and Implications for Discipleship

Drawing from the Scripture text and daily readings, what did you find challenging, encouraging, provocative, comforting, invasive, inspiring, corrective, affirming, guiding, or warning?

Shaping Intentions for Prayer

Write your discipleship intention for the week ahead.

4

WEEK

James 3:9–4:12

22

James 3:9–12

The Inestimable Power of Blessing and Cursing

With the tongue we praise our Lord and Father, and with it we curse human beings, who have been made in God's likeness. Out of the same mouth come praise and cursing. My brothers and sisters, this should not be. Can both fresh water and salt water flow from the same spring? My brothers and sisters, can a fig tree bear olives, or a grapevine bear figs? Neither can a salt spring produce fresh water.

Consider This

I am known for my discoveries of the obvious—for seeing what is often hidden in plain sight. Recently while thinking about the idea of integrity, it occurred to me that the opposite of *integrity* is dis-*integrity*. That's not exactly a real word, though. Then it hit me. *Disintegration* was the word I was looking for. When something is no longer integrated, it is disintegrated. Now, when I think of the word *disintegration*, I typically think of something being blown to smithereens. In other words, while I think of integrating as putting two or more things together into a single whole, I do not think of disintegrating something as taking them apart. Rather, I think of it as destruction. Neither the whole nor the parts exist any longer.

A person of true integrity cannot both praise God and curse people. Stated differently, a person who praises God and curses people is not a person of integrity. To praise God and curse people not only bears witness to the disintegration of your own personhood, but it also destroys the personhood of others. And while there is general application to all followers of Jesus, let's remember that James is making a specific appeal to those who want to be teachers.

Let's be clear about cursing. What we are not talking about here is using foul language. To curse someone is to do the opposite of blessing them. My friend Chris Tomlin tells a story about a middle school choir teacher who, upon listening to his voice, told him he could not sing and he should stop trying. It was a curse. Because Chris had sensed from a young age that his singing voice would be a vital part of his calling, it devastated him. If you know anything about Chris, you know that God turned this curse into an extraordinary blessing, as today he is one of the most prolific worship leaders and most sung songwriters in the world. How many others respond to a curse by damning and disqualifying themselves?

Let's press it one more step. What James is driving at is that a person who blesses God and curses people is not actually blessing God. It reminds me of the bold starkness of John in his short homily near the end of the Bible: "Anyone who claims to be in the light but hates a brother or sister is still in the darkness" (1 John 2:9).

To bless God and curse people, all of whom are made in God's image, is a non sequitur. It's as absurd as a fig tree producing olives or a freshwater spring gushing forth with salt water. Not only does it not happen; it can't happen.

Let's be mindful of and willing to assess the authenticity of our own relationship with God based on the way we bless or curse other people. I don't know about you, but I can easily drift over into cursing territory, especially in my politics. If we find ourselves cursing or unblessing other people, let's ask ourselves some hard questions and move toward some critical course corrections.

One more text for the road today: "Do not let any unwholesome talk come out of your mouths, but only what is helpful for building others up according to their needs, that it may benefit those who listen" (Ephesians 4:29).

The Prayer

God our Father, I want to be a real Christian. I know that my words will prove it one way or the other. Come, Holy Spirit, and search me and try me in this. Set a guard on my heart and order my speech. I want to bless others, not curse them. In Jesus' name. Amen.

The Questions

Can you remember a time when someone's words blessed you? How about when their words cursed you? Reflect on those experiences.

What is it like when you are around another person who talks about other people with words that effectively curse them? How about when their words bless other people?

How about you? Do you tend to be a person who blesses or curses other people with your words? Publicly? Privately? Are you grasping how cursing other people in essence negates any praise you have for God? Reflect on that a bit. Agree? Push back?

23

James 3:13–18

How to Know If You Are a Wise Person

Who is wise and understanding among you? Let them show it by their good life, by deeds done in the humility that comes from wisdom. But if you harbor bitter envy and selfish ambition in your hearts, do not boast about it or deny the truth. Such "wisdom" does not come down from heaven but is earthly, unspiritual, demonic. For where you have envy and selfish ambition, there you find disorder and every evil practice.

But the wisdom that comes from heaven is first of all pure; then peace-loving, considerate, submissive, full of mercy and good fruit, impartial and sincere. Peacemakers who sow in peace reap a harvest of righteousness.

Consider This

Who is wise and understanding among you?

It's a good question. How would you answer the question in your own circles?

Wisdom is more than good advice or sage counsel. Wisdom is not commonly associated with towering intellectual abilities. A person can be exceedingly smart, yet a thousand miles away from wise. Wisdom is not commonly associated with expertise, though it would never disdain it. Wisdom often comes as a fruit of life's experiences, though experience is not required. How often have you heard it spoken of someone that they were wise beyond their years?

Wisdom is a quality of soul. A wise person navigates life with an almost effortless gentility. A wise person tends to listen with a deep and disciplined attunement both to God and to other people. They listen far more than they talk, and they learn far more than they teach. Wisdom is being "quick to listen, slow to speak and slow to become angry" (James 1:19). Wisdom "looks intently into the perfect law that gives freedom" (v. 25) and establishes a long, slow, steady, and quiet record of doing what it says. Indeed, wisdom is a doer of the Word.

> But the wisdom that comes from heaven is first of all pure; then peace-loving, considerate, submissive, full of mercy and good fruit, impartial and sincere. Peacemakers who sow in peace reap a harvest of righteousness.

Note the stunning (and even studied) similarity of this word from James with that of his famous older brother:

> "Blessed are the poor in spirit,
>   for theirs is the kingdom of heaven.
> Blessed are those who mourn,
>   for they will be comforted.
> Blessed are the meek,
>   for they will inherit the earth.
> Blessed are those who hunger and thirst for righteousness,
>   for they will be filled.
> Blessed are the merciful,
>   for they will be shown mercy.

Blessed are the pure in heart,
  for they will see God.
Blessed are the peacemakers,
  for they will be called children of God.
Blessed are those who are persecuted because of righteousness,
  for theirs is the kingdom of heaven." (Matthew 5:3–10)

Then, on another occasion, Jesus put it this way: "For John came neither eating nor drinking, and they say, 'He has a demon.' The Son of Man came eating and drinking, and they say, 'Here is a glutton and a drunkard, a friend of tax collectors and sinners.' But wisdom is proved right by her deeds" (Matthew 11:18–19).

We don't think our way into wisdom; we act our way.

> Who is wise and understanding among you? Let them show it by their good life, by deeds done in the humility that comes from wisdom.

The authenticating signature of wisdom is a humble life. Perhaps this is why the first step toward becoming a wise person is the humility to recognize your need for it. Remember James's admonition from chapter 1? It will be a good place to stop today and an even better way to take a next step: "If any of you lacks wisdom, you should ask God" (1:5).

The Prayer

God our Father, I want to be a real Christian. Make me wise with the mind of Christ. Infuse me with the humility of Jesus and fill me with the grace to walk in it. Save me from the deception of false humility. Lead me into the real thing. In Jesus' name. Amen.

The Questions

I want to encourage you to hold up the text listed above known as the Beatitudes, Matthew 5:3–10, as a mirror. Look intently into it today and in the coming days. This is the profile of a wise person. Where do you sense the Holy Spirit calling you to grow in particular ways along these lines? Ask him.

Reflect on the way James frames the opposite of the "wisdom that comes from heaven" as demonstrated by selfish ambition and envy. Preoccupation with oneself is the enemy of wisdom. James calls it demonic. Does this concern you?

Do you aspire to be a truly humble person? How are your everyday actions proving your commitment to humility? What humble deed could you do today? Maybe even a secret one.

24

James 4:1–3

Maturity Means Moving from Managing Sin to Discipling Desires

> *What causes fights and quarrels among you? Don't they come from your desires that battle within you? You desire but do not have, so you kill. You covet but you cannot get what you want, so you quarrel and fight. You do not have because you do not ask God. When you ask, you do not receive, because you ask with wrong motives, that you may spend what you get on your pleasures.*

Consider This

One of the major moves toward maturity all of us must make is the move from managing our behavior to discipling our desires. Behavior is symptomatic of a deeper problem. That's what James is getting at with his question: "What causes fights and quarrels among you?"

James is trying to get beneath behavior to the deeper reality of our desire. Attacking behavior is like trying to put a cork in a volcano. It's like putting a Band-Aid on a staph infection. We must submit our desires to the Holy Spirit, who alone can bring our lives into alignment with the way we were made to live. The issue is not our behavior, but rather the "desires that battle within" us. Paul famously gets into this struggle in Romans 7:18–20:

> For I know that good itself does not dwell in me, that is, in my sinful nature. For I have the desire to do what is good, but I cannot carry it out. For I do not do the good I want to do, but the evil I do not want to do—this I keep on doing. Now if I do what I do not want to do, it is no longer I who do it, but it is sin living in me that does it.

Anyone who has been following Jesus for any length of time knows the reality that both James and Paul speak of. Unfortunately, most of us are willing to live in this compromised state for a long time, if not a lifetime, resigning ourselves to defeat while excusing ourselves as sinners.

Jesus did not come to earth and live a life of power over sin for us—dying to sin and rising to life in victory—only for us to live out mediocre lives of compromise. Paul continues with the diagnosis in Romans 7:21–24:

> So I find this law at work: Although I want to do good, evil is right there with me. For in my inner being I delight in God's law; but I see another law at work in me, waging war against the law of my mind and making me a prisoner of the law of sin at work within me. What a wretched man I am!

Here's where I think we go wrong: Just because something is common, we assume it's normal. Neither James nor Paul will allow it. Hear Paul out: "Who will rescue me from this body that is subject to death? Thanks be to God, who delivers me through Jesus Christ our Lord!" (Romans 7:24–25).

It gets even better:

> Therefore, there is now no condemnation for those who are in Christ Jesus, because through Christ Jesus the law of the Spirit who gives life has set you free from the law of sin and death. (Romans 8:1–2)

Discipleship means operationalizing the new reality brought about by the Holy Spirit. It's not easy. And the reason most of us get stuck here in our discipleship is that we lack the courage to be brutally honest with ourselves about the battleground of our desires that terrorize our inner lives. Beyond that, we lack the humility to be consistently honest with at least one other human being about our arrested development. I don't mean to be harsh. I'm just trying to follow Paul's lead—you know, speaking the truth in love (Ephesians 4:15).

Think about it this way: God took the Israelites out of Egypt in a single night. It took the next forty years to get Egypt out of the Israelites. Don't be discouraged and never give up. This is the good fight and we will win. Don't settle for the endless frustration of sin management. Go for the win.

The Prayer

God our Father, I want to be a real Christian. Reveal my sin to me at the deeper level of my desires. I am tired of managing behavior. I want to get to the source. Come, Holy Spirit, and search out my broken ways, so that I might be made whole and free. In Jesus' name. Amen.

The Questions

Can you identify a place of compromise with sin in your life that you have just accepted as an unwinnable struggle?

Do you see how that compromise has arrested you in your discipleship to Jesus?

Are you ready to be honest with God and yourself about this broken way at work within you? Would you dare to bring it out into the light with a close friend who will be honest with you and completely for you in the struggle?

25

James 4:4–6

Taking on the Rogue Power of Pride

> *You adulterous people, don't you know that friendship with the world means enmity against God? Therefore, anyone who chooses to be a friend of the world becomes an enemy of God. Or do you think Scripture says without reason that he jealously longs for the spirit he has caused to dwell in us? But he gives us more grace. That is why Scripture says:*
>
> *"God opposes the proud*
> *but shows favor to the humble."*

Consider This

There is more than one way to approach the meaning of many texts in the Bible. With regard to James 3 and 4, we could interpret these chapters very narrowly and assign its meaning with a high degree of specificity to the particular teachers in the community James was addressing. Think of it like an online map that can be zoomed in and out. If we zoom all the way down to the street view, we can look in on these teachers and their unique situations out of which James is calling them to repent.

If we zoom out a few clicks, we can see how the errant ways of the teachers in the church can seep into the community and cause a wider need for repentance for those who have followed the teachers' example. Again, this is why such a premium is placed on the responsibility of the teachers of God's people. A wise saying often attributed to John Maxwell holds that a person can teach anything they know but can reproduce only who they are.

Zooming out a few more clicks, we can see a bigger biblical landscape and gain an even larger scope for our understanding of the text at hand. For instance, in light of James's assertion that "friendship with the world means enmity against God," as well as the issues of "rich and poor" James raises, I am drawn to Jesus' parable of the sower. He references the seed sown in the thorny ground that springs up and seems to flourish, only to be choked out by the brambles:

> "The seed falling among the thorns refers to someone who hears the word, but the worries of this life and the deceitfulness of wealth choke the word, making it unfruitful." (Matthew 13:22)

We might turn to Jesus' instructions as recorded in John's gospel: "If the world hates you, keep in mind that it hated me first. If you belonged to the world, it would love you as its own. As it is, you do not belong to the world, but I have chosen you out of the world. That is why the world hates you" (15:18–19).

Paul's clarifying instruction also comes to mind. "Do not conform to the pattern of this world, but be transformed by the renewing of your mind" (Romans 12:2).

Then there's this matter of James in verse 5:

> Or do you think Scripture says without reason that he jealously longs for the spirit he has caused to dwell in us?

A close reading reveals that James is not talking about the work of the Holy Spirit here, but instead he means the human spirit he has put in us. God is jealous for us—for the animating dynamic of our spirit that he has put within us. I think of this spirit as the breath of life that God first breathed into Adam and Eve. Yes, he restores our spirit by work of his grace through the Holy Spirit, but we must participate.

It brings us back to this:

> But he gives us more grace. That is why Scripture says:

> "God opposes the proud
> but shows favor to the humble."

The human spirit for which God jealously longs is the seat of our desires. The Holy Spirit stands ready with the power of grace to transform our desires, but our repentance is necessary. Pride, which infects us all, turns the human spirit into a rogue force, thwarting the ways and will of God. Our pride is what tells us we can still be friends with the world and with Jesus. Our pride is the source of our self-deception.

The Prayer

God our Father, I want to be a real Christian. I know you oppose the proud, and I know I am prideful; yet I would never consider that you oppose me. Wake me up to the truth so that I might be set free. I want to be truly humble. Mold me by your mercy. In Jesus' name. Amen.

The Questions

Rate yourself. On the left end of the spectrum, put the word *humble*, and on the right end put the word *proud*. Now distribute the numbers 1 to 10 from left to right. Where do you put yourself? Are you willing to share your rating with a close friend?

How does your prideful spirit typically show up in your life? What does "friendship with the world" mean to you?

The seduction is to think we can slowly move from right to left (pride to humility) by small adjustments and slow degrees. It requires decisive intervention. What keeps you from getting on your knees before God and confessing your prideful spirit and asking for the grace of the Holy Spirit to become truly humble? Why not now? I'm going to ask us again in the next chapter.

26

James 4:7–10

How to Humble Yourself: A Step-by-Step Plan

Submit yourselves, then, to God. Resist the devil, and he will flee from you. Come near to God and he will come near to you. Wash your hands, you sinners, and purify your hearts, you double-minded. Grieve, mourn and wail. Change your laughter to mourning and your joy to gloom. Humble yourselves before the Lord, and he will lift you up.

Consider This

The questions at the end of the last chapter contained the promise that I would again raise the issue of turning away from our prideful spirit and embracing humility. The text does a masterful job without my help at all. Look at the verbs from today's text: submit, resist, come near, wash, purify, grieve, mourn, wail, change, and humble yourselves.

So when James (or anyone else in the Bible for that matter) instructs us to humble ourselves, he means this: submit, resist, come near, wash, purify, grieve, mourn, wail, change, and humble yourselves.

In other words, humility, the distinctive quality of the mind of Christ, is not something that happens in your head; it's a visceral reality. It's not thinking-oriented; it's action-based: submit, resist, come near, wash, purify, grieve, mourn, wail, change, and humble yourselves.

I'm going to cut my commentary short. James just doesn't need my help. I'm going to leave you with the text. I want you to read it again out loud. I want you to meditate on it. Pretend this text is the bone and you are the dog (I don't mean this derisively). This is actually the biblical way of meditation—getting every last bit of meat off a bone and then savoring the bone itself. Let this text lead you into a posture of humility —kneeling, lying face down on the floor, or bowing in some way. Speak words aloud to God. Write them out on paper. Ask Siri to write them down. Whatever it takes. We are dealing with the inner life here, which means we have to take extra steps to make this work tangible. James is bringing us to the altar of God.

> Submit yourselves, then, to God. Resist the devil, and he will flee from you. Come near to God and he will come near to you. Wash your hands, you sinners, and purify your hearts, you double-minded. Grieve, mourn and wail. Change your laughter to mourning and your joy to gloom. Humble yourselves before the Lord, and he will lift you up.

The Prayer

God our Father, I want to be a real Christian. I want to walk in the path of submitting to your Holy Spirit, resisting the devil, and drawing near to your throne of grace, of being washed and purified. Teach me to grieve, mourn, and wail, that I might change and become truly humble. In short, I want to be like Jesus. In his name I pray. Amen.

The Questions

Which verbs in this list jump out at you?

a. submit
b. resist
c. come near
d. wash
e. purify
f. grieve
g. mourn
h. wail
i. change
j. humble yourselves

What might it mean for you to "resist the devil"?

Are you ready to humble yourself in the sight of the Lord? Where might you go—a hidden and solitary place—to do this? Mark the day in some way so that you can remember it going forward. Put down a stake. Pick up a rock. Write down the date and your memory of what you did. Whatever it takes.

27 James 4:11–12

How to Stop Talking About People

Brothers and sisters, do not slander one another. Anyone who speaks against a brother or sister or judges them speaks against the law and judges it. When you judge the law, you are not keeping it, but sitting in judgment on it. There is only one Lawgiver and Judge, the one who is able to save and destroy. But you—who are you to judge your neighbor?

Consider This

I do it. You do it. We all do it. Let's just get this out of the way. We all talk about other people. And talking about other people is not really the issue; the issue is slandering them.

There's the legal idea of slander, which means speaking an untruth about another person that results in damage to their reputation. Then there's the biblical idea of slander, which means speaking ill of another person. If I speak ill of you and it damages your reputation and you sue me in civil court, there is a way out for me. I can prove that what I said about you was true. Honesty is so often how we justify speaking ill of other people. We consider that what we are saying is true; hence, it is not slanderous. We simply think of it as truth-telling. Of course, there is the small problem of talking *about* people instead of talking *to* them, but the truth is the truth, right?

As best as I can tell, there is no defense for the kind of slander that James references. Regardless of whether what you say about another person is true or not, to speak ill of them is to slander. What is James's rationale? For James, to speak ill of another person means to judge them, and for James (and for us too), there is only one judge—God. To judge another person means to put oneself in the position of God. God, as the Lawgiver, is the only one capable of judging human beings. The role of a human being is to simply be a doer of the Word rather than a judger of other people on whether they are doing or not doing the

Word. According to God's Word, when we step into the role of judging other people, we step out of our role as a neighbor and usurp the role of God over them. This is wrong for anyone to do, and it's particularly egregious when teachers do it. This is not a shooting foul for James. He seems prepared to eject someone from the game for slandering others.

So we are back to the issue of our words and their power to create or destroy. I don't know about you, but this text convicts me. In our day-to-day work, family, and community life, we can't help but discuss other people. Sure, it's a good practice to not speak of another person who is not actually present, but it's just going to happen. We have conversations at work with our coworkers about our bosses, and with our bosses about our coworkers. We quite naturally process our conflicts with people by bringing others alongside to discuss them. Sure, there's always the possibility of politely walking away from such conversations that are about a person who is not present, but I think there may well be a more practical and reasonable approach.

When I'm in a situation where another person is being discussed in a difficult way, here's my approach: I will be willing to discuss the matter at hand, but I will refuse to speak ill of the person being discussed. I will not feel the need to defend the person not present, but I will call the foul if the conversation moves toward speaking ill of them as a person. If the conversation turns toward judging a person's motives and such, I will be the one in the conversation who will push back against this line of conversation and advocate that the issue be taken up personally with them.

Here's the kicker: If I'm in a conversation where another person is being slandered and I choose to be silent, I am complicit in the slander. My choices are to walk away or to defend the reputation of the person not present. The latter is the courageous choice. To defend a person's reputation is not to take their side in a conflict; it is to stand in their stead as a fellow human being and protect them from injury or harm, from being defamed and disparaged.

The Prayer

God our Father, I want to be a real Christian. Prick my spirit at the first impulse of slandering others. Give me the courage to stand up for those who are being slandered outside of their hearing. Help me to become the kind of person who graciously protects the reputation of those not present. In Jesus' name. Amen.

The Questions

What is it in us that makes us want to jump on the conversational bandwagon when the subject of a person who is not present comes up?

Are you grasping the difference between talking constructively and objectively about people in the context of everyday life situations and talking about them in ways that damage their reputation? Remember, just because it may be true is no defense for sitting in judgment.

Try this mantra on for size: "I'm not the judge." "I'm not the judge." "I'm not the judge." If your name came up in a conversation among others and it turned to personal attacks and ill speaking, wouldn't you want someone there to stand up for you? How does thinking like this impact the way you'll act when a conversation about someone begins to take place in your presence?

Week 4:
Discussion Questions

Hearing the Text: Read James 3:9–4:12

With the tongue we praise our Lord and Father, and with it we curse human beings, who have been made in God's likeness. Out of the same mouth come praise and cursing. My brothers and sisters, this should not be. Can both fresh water and salt water flow from the same spring? My brothers and sisters, can a fig tree bear olives, or a grapevine bear figs? Neither can a salt spring produce fresh water.

Who is wise and understanding among you? Let them show it by their good life, by deeds done in the humility that comes from wisdom. But if you harbor bitter envy and selfish ambition in your hearts, do not boast about it or deny the truth. Such "wisdom" does not come down from heaven but is earthly, unspiritual, demonic. For where you have envy and selfish ambition, there you find disorder and every evil practice.

But the wisdom that comes from heaven is first of all pure; then peace-loving, considerate, submissive, full of mercy and good fruit, impartial and sincere. Peacemakers who sow in peace reap a harvest of righteousness.

What causes fights and quarrels among you? Don't they come from your desires that battle within you? You desire but do not have, so you kill. You covet but you cannot get what you want, so you quarrel and fight. You do not have because you do not ask God. When you ask, you do not receive, because you ask with wrong motives, that you may spend what you get on your pleasures.

You adulterous people, don't you know that friendship with the world means enmity against God? Therefore, anyone who chooses to be a friend of the world becomes an enemy of God. Or do you think

Scripture says without reason that he jealously longs for the spirit he has caused to dwell in us? But he gives us more grace. That is why Scripture says:

> "God opposes the proud
> but shows favor to the humble."

Submit yourselves, then, to God. Resist the devil, and he will flee from you. Come near to God and he will come near to you. Wash your hands, you sinners, and purify your hearts, you double-minded. Grieve, mourn and wail. Change your laughter to mourning and your joy to gloom. Humble yourselves before the Lord, and he will lift you up.

Brothers and sisters, do not slander one another. Anyone who speaks against a brother or sister or judges them speaks against the law and judges it. When you judge the law, you are not keeping it, but sitting in judgment on it. There is only one Lawgiver and Judge, the one who is able to save and destroy. But you—who are you to judge your neighbor?

Responding to the Text

- What did you hear?
- What did you see?
- What did you otherwise sense from the Lord?

Sharing Insights and Implications for Discipleship

Drawing from the Scripture text and daily readings, what did you find challenging, encouraging, provocative, comforting, invasive, inspiring, corrective, affirming, guiding, or warning?

Shaping Intentions for Prayer

Write your discipleship intention for the week ahead.

5

WEEK

James 4:13–5:20

29

James 4:13–17

How to Not Be an Arrogant Person

Now listen, you who say, "Today or tomorrow we will go to this or that city, spend a year there, carry on business and make money." Why, you do not even know what will happen tomorrow. What is your life? You are a mist that appears for a little while and then vanishes. Instead, you ought to say, "If it is the Lord's will, we will live and do this or that." As it is, you boast in your arrogant schemes. All such boasting is evil. If anyone, then, knows the good they ought to do and doesn't do it, it is sin for them.

Consider This

Through the years, some commentators on James have opined that this is an antibusiness or antimoneymaking text. Others have tried to argue that James somehow pits human planning against the will of God. Neither of these interpretations has merit. James is not dealing with money and commerce here. He is not making a statement that human planning is somehow incongruent with following the will of God. James is dealing with the pervasive problem of human pride and presumption.

James is taking on the mentality that would say, "I am in charge. I am the captain of my own ship. I control my destiny. I can do what I want, when I want, however I want, and for however long I want with whomever I want."

Watch for it in the text:

> Today or tomorrow [whenever I want] we [with whomever I want] will go to this or that city [wherever I want], spend a year there [for however long I want], carry on business [doing whatever I want] and make money [for whatever purpose I want].

This kind of rhetoric sounds strikingly familiar to the kinds of claims a candidate for political office or a billionaire businessperson might make. Making plans is good. Making money is good. Making yourself the captain of your own ship—not so much. At least this is not the way for the followers of Jesus. The world will be the world. We can predict it and expect it; we just can't imitate it. Our options are arrogance or humility, and there's nothing worse than arrogance. James brings us back around to the core dynamic of the disciple of Jesus—namely, humility.

> What is your life? You are a mist that appears for a little while and then vanishes.

Humility does not mean thinking less of yourself; it means having a proper estimation of yourself. It does not come from self-abnegation, but rather from keen self-awareness. It's one of the great gifts of Ash Wednesday each year for those who observe it. We kneel at the altar, a cross is traced on our forehead in ashes and oil, and these gracious words are spoken over us: "From dust you have come and to dust you shall return. Repent and believe the gospel."

This is a call to humility, which means embracing the frailty, fragility, and finitude of our existence. We are glorious dust. I am glorious dust. You are glorious dust. To repent means renouncing arrogance, presumption, and proud self-determination over and over again until they lose their foothold in our lives. If we can come to own the truth about our lives, our lives will become an ever-increasing glorious expression of the truth of the love of God.

> Instead, you ought to say, "If it is the Lord's will, we will live and do this or that."

Deo volente—"Lord willing." More than the utterance of words, this phrase is a cultivated disposition of the disciple's deepest self. It is a happy declaration that God sees all, knows all, and has our very best interests at heart in all things. He is able to do abundantly above and beyond anything we could think, ask, or even imagine (see Ephesians 3:20).

Let us seek the Holy Spirit's intervention in our spirit to help us become brilliantly unassuming and patiently submissive while we go about our wise planning, holding everything in joyful trust before the God who has entrusted himself to us.

> Why, you do not even know what will happen tomorrow.

Okay, I know it's a cheesy cliché, but it's true. Write it down. "I don't know what tomorrow holds, but I do know who holds tomorrow."

The Prayer

God our Father, I want to be a real Christian. I know that means humility. I struggle here in ways beyond my awareness. Reveal to me the subtleties of my pride. Show me the arrogance I am unaware of. Forgive me for presuming on your will. Come, Holy Spirit, and teach me submission to Jesus. In Jesus' name. Amen.

The Questions

Arrogance comes from pride; pride comes from insecurity, which comes from the deep-seated need to cover over internal brokenness or woundedness by projecting a false self. Interact with that statement.

What keeps you in an anxious state about the future and causes you to need to be in control? What would you have to believe about God in your deepest self in order to release control?

What would it mean to ask God to inspire your planning from the beginning instead of asking God to bless the plans you have come up with in the end? How can you move in that direction today?

What would repentance from self-determination and self-will look like for you? How will you reckon with it?

30

James 5:1–6

How Self-Indulgence Wins and How It Loses

Now listen, you rich people, weep and wail because of the misery that is coming on you. Your wealth has rotted, and moths have eaten your clothes. Your gold and silver are corroded. Their corrosion will testify against you and eat your flesh like fire. You have hoarded wealth in the last days. Look! The wages you failed to pay the workers who mowed your fields are crying out against you. The cries of the harvesters have reached the ears of the Lord Almighty. You have lived on earth in luxury and self-indulgence. You have fattened yourselves in the day of slaughter. You have condemned and murdered the innocent one, who was not opposing you.

Consider This

This may be the most stinging passage in James's whole letter. He references an absolute reversal of fortune for the rich. They have gone from mountains of money with lives of luxury and self-indulgence to rotting wealth, moth-eaten clothes, and corroded gold and silver. When James wrote, "You have lived on earth in luxury and self-indulgence," he may have been reflecting on the words of his brother Jesus:

> "Do not store up for yourselves treasures on earth, where moths and vermin destroy, and where thieves break in and steal. But store up for yourselves treasures in heaven, where moths and vermin do not destroy, and where thieves do not break in and steal. For where your treasure is, there your heart will be also." (Matthew 6:19–21)

It's easy for me to think of people who have a lot more than I do when it comes to texts like these. My mind wants to turn to those who own multiple houses, have all the toys, take all the trips, and stay in all the best places. It's precisely the wrong move when it comes to texts like these. James does not want us to call to mind the proverbial 1 percent. He wants the slideshow running through our minds to turn to refugees driven from their homes and country, children sold into slavery, widows, orphans, single moms, the mentally ill, the imprisoned, the aging and alone, and so forth. James wants us to be convicted about the way we judge the poor for the money they spend on cigarettes and lottery tickets as we flash our Starbucks gift card at the register in exchange for yet another five-dollar latte.

The rich aren't people who have more than we do. If you are reading this reflection, chances are you're included in the rich category—at least I'm coming to grips with this for myself. I absolutely hate writing about the perils of riches—probably more than my readers hate reading about it. But just as we welcome the encouragement that comes from the Word of God, we must open ourselves to its confrontation and critique.

So what are we to do? The easy thing is to endure the brief storm of self-shaming that inevitably comes from such confrontation. We can feel bad about what we have, the relative luxury in which we live, and the seductive self-indulgence of our lifestyles. The truth? That will accomplish nothing of consequence. Repentance has much less to do with how bad we feel about ourselves and much more to do with how bad we feel about the brokenness of others. Repentance doesn't so much look like me selling my stuff so I can give the money to the poor—though that is not a bad thing—as it looks like everyday, responsible relationships with people in need. It's not about keeping my self-indulgence in check; it's about learning to give myself away. When I begin to love people in need as I love myself, self-indulgence will take care of itself.

The Prayer

God our Father, I want to be a real Christian. Reorient my repentance, not around how I feel about myself, but around how I fail to love others. Forgive my sense of nobility in my efforts to help the poor; lead me instead to love the poor. In fact, help me see and love them, not as the poor, but as I love myself. In Jesus' name. Amen.

The Questions

So how about it? Have you come to grips with the fact that you might be in the category of the rich? Will you consider that?

Do you understand how fighting against self-indulgence actually plays into self-indulgence's greatest strategy—keeping the focus on ourselves?

Are you in real relationships with people living in poverty or otherwise in need? Not primarily as a benefactor, but as friends? What might it look like to move in that direction?

31

James 5:7–9

Why *Wait* Is Not a Four-Letter Word

Be patient, then, brothers and sisters, until the Lord's coming. See how the farmer waits for the land to yield its valuable crop, patiently waiting for the autumn and spring rains. You too, be patient and stand firm, because the Lord's coming is near. Don't grumble against one another, brothers and sisters, or you will be judged. The Judge is standing at the door!

Consider This

No one wants to wait. There is nothing like waiting to remind us of our powerlessness to control a situation.

Remember our context. James is writing to a group of Jewish Christians in Jerusalem who have been living under the oppression and abuse perpetrated by the rich, presumably unconverted and unrepentant Jews in the city. Throughout the letter, James has instructed the little church to resist the temptation to resort to violence against their oppressors. In today's text, James reassures them that the judgment of God is coming soon against their enemies.

Indeed, within decades, God's judgment came in the form of the Roman army that destroyed the city of Jerusalem. It was an unthinkable catastrophe of epic proportions. It turns out James was exactly right:

> The Judge is standing at the door!

Jesus gave the same warning when he said, "Not one stone here will be left on another," in speaking of this judgment (Matthew 24:2).

In the face of trial, testing, suffering, and hardship, we face two primary temptations. First, we want to fight back against our enemies. Retaliation inevitably leads to escalation, which turns to outright war. Second, under the stress and strain of the situation, we easily find ourselves turning against one another. It begins with grumbling that leads to dissension and finally to division.

James reminds us of the promise of God and instructs us in the ways of God:

> You too, be patient and stand firm, because the Lord's coming is near.

Paul would say the same kind of thing to the Christians being persecuted in Rome: "Do not take revenge, my dear friends, but leave room for God's wrath, for it is written: 'It is mine to avenge; I will repay,' says the Lord" (Romans 12:19).

We do not retaliate, but rather we forgive, which is another way of saying we refuse to fight back. We do not return wrong for wrong. We trust in God's judgment and the sign of our trust—patient waiting.

Not only is waiting a sign of trust, but it is a mark of courage as well. The psalmist urges us, "Wait for the Lord; be strong and take heart and wait for the Lord" (Psalm 27:14).

David gives a vivid picture of the faithfulness of God in the face of our waiting:

> I waited patiently for the Lord;
> he turned to me and heard my cry.
> He lifted me out of the slimy pit,

out of the mud and mire;
he set my feet on a rock
and gave me a firm place to stand.
He put a new song in my mouth,
a hymn of praise to our God.
Many will see and fear the LORD
and put their trust in him. (Psalm 40:1–3)

No one wants to wait. There is nothing like waiting that reminds us of our powerlessness to control a situation; and there is nothing like waiting that reminds us of who is in control. Far from a passive approach, waiting on the Lord holds the source of our greatest possibilities—trusting God.

The Prayer

God our Father, I want to be a real Christian. I know this means letting go of my need to be in control of situations and people. Teach me the patience of waiting on you, even in situations where it seems I am waiting on people. Come, Holy Spirit, and fill me with the fruit of patient love. No more fretting in anxiety. In Jesus' name. Amen.

The Questions

Why do we hate to wait? What is underneath our disdain for waiting on the Lord?

How is waiting an antidote to taking revenge? Are you in the midst of or do you recall a situation where you faced the choice of retaliating for a wrong done to you or trusting in the Lord by waiting on him to act? Which way did you go? What did you learn?

Does waiting feel like cowardice or courage to you? Where do you find yourself most out of control of the outcomes in your life at the moment? How might you reorient your approach?

32

James 5:10–12

Combating Evil Instead of Trying to Explain It

Brothers and sisters, as an example of patience in the face of suffering, take the prophets who spoke in the name of the Lord. As you know, we count as blessed those who have persevered. You have heard of Job's perseverance and have seen what the Lord finally brought about. The Lord is full of compassion and mercy.

Above all, my brothers and sisters, do not swear—not by heaven or by earth or by anything else. All you need to say is a simple "Yes" or "No." Otherwise you will be condemned.

Consider This

On the one hand, James comes off like a prizefighter. He has mastered the art of jab, jab, jab, and then the right hook you never saw coming. On the other hand, he can work with the deftness of a skilled trial lawyer. For instance, as he continues his exhortation about not taking revenge and waiting on the Lord's judgment, he calls the proverbial surprise witness—Job. And Job turns out to be not only a surprise witness, but a star witness.

It's like he's saying to the little band of weary Christians in Jerusalem, "So you think *you've* got it bad? You think *you* are dealing with some pretty big injustices? Your Honor, the prosecution would like to call Job to the witness stand."

He could have called Jeremiah, Ezekiel, Isaiah, or any number of prophets who took their share of undeserved scorn and persecution. Not James. James presents the worst-case scenario—the worst of the worst apparent injustices in the history of injustices.

In case you are new to Job, through no fault of his own he lost his seven sons, three daughters, seven thousand sheep, three thousand camels, five hundred yoke of oxen, five hundred female donkeys, and all of his servants—in the span of a single day. If that weren't enough, he then came down with something that looked like a cross between skin cancer and shingles. And to top it all off, his good friends showed up and castigated him with blame for the situation for days on end.

Why call Job to the stand? Because Job patiently suffered all of it without losing faith in God. Job took the long view. To be sure, Job protested. He cried out in frustration and angst, but through it all he never let go of God because he knew God would never let go of him. James isn't sitting around asking, *Why do bad things happen to good people?* In fact, this question that wrecks the faith of so many people today isn't even asked in Scripture, much less answered. Of course bad things happen to good people. In a world as corrupt and fallen as ours is, something bad is going to happen to someone good every single day. Throughout the course of history, the followers of Jesus have spent far more time combating evil than trying to explain it.

The last thing a person can afford to do in the midst of a dark trial is to give up on God. James reminds us to take the long view. Don't be afraid to cry out to God in angst and even anger. Lament and grieve in his presence, but never ever give up. Never ever let go. Remind yourself that the Judge stands at the door. No matter how bad you have it, Job had it worse.

Finally, we need to be reminded that patience in the face of suffering is not simply giving in or resigning oneself to circumstances. Patience is a fruit of the Holy Spirit—a deep inward supernatural disposition that arises from abandoning oneself to God in the midst of the trial.

The Prayer

God our Father, I want to be a real Christian. Only you can hold me together when everything else is falling apart. Train my disposition to ask not "why me?" but "why not me?" Let hard times and trials teach me perseverance and even joy because of how close it draws me to you. Let me learn from James, Job, Jesus, and anyone else who has walked this hard trail. In Jesus' name. Amen.

The Questions

Has it ever occurred to you to consider Job in the midst of a difficult trial or season of loss in your life?

How much have you struggled with the *Why do bad things happen to good people?* question? What would it mean to adopt more of a posture of combating evil than struggling with the injustice of it?

How about patience in the face of hardship and suffering? Are you ready for a patience that comes from a deeper place than your own inner efforts? Have you witnessed this Holy Spirit–infused patience in another person in a difficult trial? What do you observe about them?

33

James 5:13–18

The Difference Between the Power of Prayer and the Power of the People Praying

Is anyone among you in trouble? Let them pray. Is anyone happy? Let them sing songs of praise. Is anyone among you sick? Let them call the elders of the church to pray over them and anoint them with oil in the name of the Lord. And the prayer offered in faith will make the sick person well; the Lord will raise them up. If they have sinned, they will be forgiven. Therefore confess your sins to each other and pray for each other so that you may be healed. The prayer of a righteous person is powerful and effective.

Elijah was a human being, even as we are. He prayed earnestly that it would not rain, and it did not rain on the land for three and a half years. Again he prayed, and the heavens gave rain, and the earth produced its crops.

Consider This

We often hear this phrase bandied about: "I believe in the power of prayer." It's as though a practice or an activity holds power in and of itself. Prayer, in and of itself, holds no power. God holds the power. We might be wiser to say, "I believe in the power of God." So where does this leave prayer? Is it our prayers that somehow access and appropriate the power of God? I don't think that's it either.

Another mistaken approach often made is the way prayer is said to be contingent on the faith of the person being prayed for. In other words, people will assert that a person is not healed because they didn't have enough faith. Today's passage reverses this understanding. What if it's not so much the faith of the one being prayed for that determines the outcome but instead the faith of the one doing the praying? And what if by the term *faith* we don't necessarily mean the level of sincere belief held by the person praying at the time of the prayer? What if the effectiveness of prayer is somehow related to the nature of the character of the person praying? I think this is what James is saying to us here.

> Is anyone among you sick? Let them call the elders of the church to pray over them and anoint them with oil in the name of the Lord.

Why would James urge us to call on the elders of the church? We should note that our best understanding of James in its original context shows that James is not referring to elders in the sense of persons holding a particular office, role, or responsibility in the church; he is referring to people in the community who bore a distinctive kind of godly character —people who possessed a quality of holiness that was powerful to witness yet hidden from themselves. These were the ones the sick wanted to invoke the name of Jesus and the power of the Holy Spirit over them when they were sick. Understand, though, that they were not sought out because they had a special gifting or secret knowledge. These elders were sought out because they were full of God. These elders were the kind of people in whom the fullness of God was pleased to dwell, people in whom the Holy Spirit had unfettered access, and people through whom the love of Jesus Christ could flow in creative power to heal, restore, and bring life. In all probability, James is not talking about elders who were ordained by the bishop. In today's parlance, they would likely more often than not fit into the typically unhelpful designation of "laypeople."

While such ordained elders could certainly qualify for this responsibility, they cannot hold exclusive rights to it. In my understanding, while the elders of a community may include the ordained, they can never be limited to the ordained. Elders are men and women whose lives exude the holiness of Jesus because all of their confidence is in him and not in themselves. They cannot be spotted by their credentials, but rather by the deep consecration of their lives to God and others. I think it's why James says:

> The prayer of a righteous person is powerful and effective.

Permit me a short, tangential rabbit trail. In the ways of God, it's never the office, role, or position that legitimizes the person or their authority or power. It's the other way around. It's the authentic, godly character of the person who legitimizes the authority of the position. For instance, ordination does not somehow magically confer authority on the one ordained. It can create positional power, privilege, and responsibility, but true authority is the gift of the Holy Spirit and is mostly conferred on the humble. When a person is ordained, the bishop instructs the ordained to take authority. And as best as I can understand, these people are being urged not to somehow grasp or possess power as much as to become a particular kind of person—the kind of person the Holy Spirit can trust with the authority of Jesus.

To put the exclamation on his point about the kind of people whose prayers God answers, James calls a final witness—the prophet Elijah.

> Elijah was a human being, even as we are. He prayed earnestly that it would not rain, and it did not rain on the land for three and a half years. Again he prayed, and the heavens gave rain, and the earth produced its crops.

Enough said.

The Prayer

God our Father, I want to be a real Christian. I don't want to hide behind a role, position, or job title. I want my life to reflect the authority of the love of Jesus. I want the kind of authority that is recognized by others because they recognize you in me. Come, Holy Spirit, and train my spirit to walk in this way of wisdom. In Jesus' name. Amen.

The Questions

How do you react to the nuance between the power of prayer and the power of God, and the powerful and effective prayers of a righteous person? Flesh that out in your own words.

Do you know any elders in the sense that James speaks of elders? Describe them. What do they have in common?

Do you aspire, in humility of course, to become the kind of person who James would refer to as an elder? Why? Why not?

34

James 5:19–20

Thank You, James: A Parting Gift from the Brother of Jesus

> *My brothers and sisters, if one of you should wander from the truth and someone should bring that person back, remember this: whoever turns a sinner from the error of their way will save them from death and cover over a multitude of sins.*

Consider This

There's a line in one of the favorite hymns of the church that jars me every time I sing it. The line comes in the third and final verse of "Come, Thou Fount of Every Blessing."

O to grace how great a debtor
daily I'm constrained to be!
Let thy goodness, like a fetter,
bind my wandering heart to thee.
Prone to wander, Lord, I feel it,
prone to leave the God I love;
here's my heart, O take and seal it,
seal it for thy courts above.

I didn't know until recently that certain churches will not sing the third verse as it was written. They have taken the liberty to change the lyrics, omitting the words *wandering* and *prone to wander*, and replacing them with another idea entirely. I don't want to mischaracterize their clearly convicted point of view, but they seem to hold to a position that there is a threshold of holiness, and once crossed, it cannot abide or admit even the possibility of a "proneness" to wander away from God.

Not James. While he believes in the possibility of a pure and even rarified holiness, he will not release his respect for the seductive power of sin and the ever-present propensity of the self-deceiving ways of our race.

> My brothers and sisters, if one of you should wander from the truth and someone should bring that person back . . .

So what does James mean by "wander from the truth"? I don't think he means to decisively walk away from God. The context of the passage indicates he is talking about sin. While we are granted power over sin and gifted by the Spirit to put sin to death and live lives free from its hold, I'm not sure we are ever given immunity from its infectious reach.

Though we are in remission or even completely cured, the cancer of sin can always come back. We need not live in fear of its return, but rather we can live in awe of the ever-present, every day mercy of God to uphold, preserve, and protect us from sin's reach. It harkens back to our long and humbling obedience to the ancient declaration of faith known as the Jesus Prayer: "Lord Jesus Christ, Son of God, have mercy on me, a sinner." The mercy I most need as a sinner is not the comfortable assurance of repeat forgiveness for failure, but the humility to constantly know my desperate need of Jesus to save me from presuming on his grace.

The last hard truth James offers us is this one: We don't typically wander away from God by means of a willful decision. We wander away from God when we lose ourselves in the shifting shadows and seductive shades of sin. While I think that for me to leave the God I love is highly unlikely, I do know of my proneness to wander into sin. What I must realize is that the latter, unguarded by myself and unchecked by others, almost always leads to the former. It's why James puts a premium on the necessity of watching over one another in love.

> Whoever turns a sinner from the error of their way will save them from death and cover over a multitude of sins.

It's like my friend Ricky once aptly said to me, "If I was driving by your house and it was on fire, would you want me to tell you?"

Thank you, James, for the courage to sniff out the smoke from the still-smoldering sin in our lives and to let us know. Thank you, brother of Jesus and brother of ours, for refusing to protect us from his truth so that we might never be shielded from his grace.

Thank you, James.

The Prayer

God our Father, I want to be a real Christian. I know you have saved me, yet I know you are still saving me. Sin has no power over me, yet I still stumble at times. I am in constant need of your mercy and grace. Forgive my ways of wandering away from this truth. And make me the kind of person that those who are wandering away will trust. Let me, like you, never let go of them. In Jesus' name. Amen.

The Questions

How about you? Are you in touch with your proneness to wander away from God and into sin? How do you deal with that? Where do you go with it?

Do you have a James kind of person in your life or in your past? Has anyone ever helped you turn from sin and the error of your ways? Have you ever served another person in this fashion? What do you remember about that? What did you learn? Have you given permission to others to do this for you if needed? Will you?

In what particular ways do you want to say thank you to James?

Week 5: Discussion Questions

Hearing the Text: Read James 4:13–5:20

Now listen, you who say, "Today or tomorrow we will go to this or that city, spend a year there, carry on business and make money." Why, you do not even know what will happen tomorrow. What is your life? You are a mist that appears for a little while and then vanishes. Instead, you ought to say, "If it is the Lord's will, we will live and do this or that." As it is, you boast in your arrogant schemes. All such boasting is evil. If anyone, then, knows the good they ought to do and doesn't do it, it is sin for them.

Now listen, you rich people, weep and wail because of the misery that is coming on you. Your wealth has rotted, and moths have eaten your clothes. Your gold and silver are corroded. Their corrosion will testify against you and eat your flesh like fire. You have hoarded wealth in the last days. Look! The wages you failed to pay the workers who mowed your fields are crying out against you. The cries of the harvesters have reached the ears of the Lord Almighty. You have lived on earth in luxury and self-indulgence. You have fattened yourselves in the day of slaughter. You have condemned and murdered the innocent one, who was not opposing you.

Be patient, then, brothers and sisters, until the Lord's coming. See how the farmer waits for the land to yield its valuable crop, patiently waiting for the autumn and spring rains. You too, be patient and stand firm, because the Lord's coming is near. Don't grumble against one another, brothers and sisters, or you will be judged. The Judge is standing at the door!

Brothers and sisters, as an example of patience in the face of suffering, take the prophets who spoke in the name of the Lord. As you know, we count as blessed those who have persevered. You have heard of Job's perseverance and have seen what the Lord finally brought about. The Lord is full of compassion and mercy.

Above all, my brothers and sisters, do not swear—not by heaven or by earth or by anything else. All you need to say is a simple "Yes" or "No." Otherwise you will be condemned.

Is anyone among you in trouble? Let them pray. Is anyone happy? Let them sing songs of praise. Is anyone among you sick? Let them call the elders of the church to pray over them and anoint them with oil in the name of the Lord. And the prayer offered in faith will make the sick person well; the Lord will raise them up. If they have sinned, they will be forgiven. Therefore confess your sins to each other and pray for each other so that you may be healed. The prayer of a righteous person is powerful and effective.

Elijah was a human being, even as we are. He prayed earnestly that it would not rain, and it did not rain on the land for three and a half years. Again he prayed, and the heavens gave rain, and the earth produced its crops.

My brothers and sisters, if one of you should wander from the truth and someone should bring that person back, remember this: Whoever turns a sinner from the error of their way will save them from death and cover over a multitude of sins.

Responding to the Text

- What did you hear?
- What did you see?
- What did you otherwise sense from the Lord?

Sharing Insights and Implications for Discipleship

Drawing from the Scripture text and daily readings, what did you find challenging, encouraging, provocative, comforting, invasive, inspiring, corrective, affirming, guiding, or warning?

Shaping Intentions for Prayer

Write your discipleship intention for the week ahead.

Conclusion/Charge

Every Sunday in my little church in Gillett, Arkansas, I invite the children to come down for a short message from me to them. I always ask them this question: "How do you punch the devil?" They respond with exuberance, "By saying God's Word!" The adults in the background join in as well. I want these children (and their families) to learn to love God's Word.

It's what I love so much about James. I would call James an apostle of the Word. He is a straight-shooting, hard-hitting, no-nonsense witness of Jesus. As we said at the beginning of this journey, James just might be the first real Christian. We aren't even through the first chapter when he cuts to the chase of his whole message:

> Do not merely listen to the word, and so deceive yourselves. Do what it says. (James 1:22)

The activist reader of Scripture considers this their trump card when it comes to their frustrations with the contemplative reader of the Bible. "Be doers of the Word and not just hearers," they retort. And they are right. And they are wrong.

When it comes to the Word of God, James cannot be confined to either category. He is neither a contemplative reader nor an activist reader. I would call James a comprehensivist reader. You must listen deeply, and you must act demonstrably. It is not either/or, but rather both/and.

It's why some years back I created a rubric for a comprehensive approach to the Word of God. It is a mnemonic device utilizing the four fingers and thumb of one's hand with each of the five dimensions working in an alliterative fashion—beginning with the letter *R*. You might even want to trace out your hand on a piece of paper and insert the words into the corresponding fingers.

The Five *R*s of "Saying God's Word"

Read Aloud (pinky finger)
Focus on hearing the Word coming from the voice of God through your voice.
Ruminate/Meditate (ring finger) As you read through a second time, underline or highlight the word(s) and/or phrase(s) that capture your attention. Invite the Holy Spirit to turn them over in your heart and mind as you dwell on them. Jot down any thoughts and insights.
Rememberize (middle finger)
Write down any particular portion that seems to invite some sustained attention.
Research (index finger)
Note any questions or curiosities the text raises that you'd like to return to later for further study.
Rehearse (thumb)
How might the Scripture be shaping a demonstration of the Word in your own heart, home, church, and city? In other words, how might you practice or do it?

I have a faint memory of a cartoon strip from my childhood. Many of you will remember *Peanuts* by Charles Schultz and its starring characters, the inimitable Charlie Brown and his friends Linus and Lucy. In the cartoon strip, I recall Lucy balling up her hand into a tight fist as she tells Linus to change the TV channel, reminding him that her five fingers individually aren't much, but when they curl together, they turn into a scary weapon. Linus looks at his hand, palm open and fingers stretched out, and asks, "Why can't you guys get organized like that?"

Now try making a fist with your four fingers and striking something soft nearby to see how it works. It's a fail. Now let your thumb wrap around those fingers, squeeze them tight and try striking the soft nearby object. The thumb brings something of a miraculous transformation to the otherwise clumsy disorganization of the four fingers. It's why that fifth *R* is the thumb. When we become doers (rehearsers) of the Word of God and not just readers, ruminators, rememberizers, and researchers, it all comes together into a powerful punch.

So how do you punch the devil? Yep, by saying God's Word—in every possible way. This is the pathway to becoming a real Christian. Thanks for joining me on this pathway.

I welcome you to join me on the Wake-Up Call every morning where we do this work together every single day: Seedbed.com/wakeupcall. I look forward to seeing you on the field.

For the Awakening,

John David "J. D." Walt Jr.,
founder and sower-in-chief,
Seedbed, Inc.

WAKE-UP CALL

by SEEDBED

Knowing Jesus Better Every Day

WITH J. D. WALT

Subscribe Today!

SEEDBED.COM/WAKEUPCALL

Spotify

Podcasts

YouTube

DAILY SEEDS

with J. D. Walt

A different kind of Bible Study!

It's time to focus more on knowing Jesus than knowing about Jesus.